Praise for Saniel ~~and his Way of Waki~~

"If you're looking for freedom, if you sense there's more – to you and to life – that you're longing to connect with, if you're interested in a profound teaching of truth that is within reach, read this book. Saniel Bonder has given a great gift to us all."
Mercedes Kirkel, 42, editor, dancer, mother

"I am 68 years old. I had studied with two teachers and taken innumerable seminars, but I'd given up hope for my own awakening. I was under the impression that self-realization would either take a long time, or was practically impossible. When I met Saniel, I was impressed and moved by how quickly people around him were awakening. After working with him for about a year and a half, much to my astonishment, I awoke! If I can do it, anyone can."
Richard Brumm, former engineer and pilot, father

"As a psychotherapist, I have explored and experienced change in my human character. As a spiritual practitioner, I have entered into classic samadhi states and realizations of consciousness. Still, until I encountered Saniel's work, I did not feel rested as myself, conscious and free from disturbing separations in my nature and with others. Within a short time in my practice with Saniel, the traditional goal of analysis – deep ego integration – and the goal of traditional spirituality – conscious abiding as the Divine Self – became mine. Saniel's teaching is a very real evolution of the traditions, more effective than any other work I know."
Sandra Glickman, MFCC, 58

"The guiding principle of my own search has been this: never accept a spiritual path that denies the practical, tangible realities of our nature. I have investigated many paths, but only in Saniel's work have I realized a true liberation that embraces the full integrity of my own existence. If you yearn to live in freedom, and are willing to discover the responsible truths of embodied living, then I urge you to read this book!"
Jon Mattingly, 28, growth facilitator

"A massage therapist and mother, also a survivor of alcoholism, divorce, and a near-fatal car accident, I'm an average American woman. Recognizing myself to be Consciousness embodied as me, I prove that Saniel Bonder's work of Waking Down in mutuality is accessible to everyday human beings."
Sharon Schlotthauer, 50

"This work is about personal freedom through liberation from self-imposed limits, and about living responsibly in relationship. I came into it as a novice spiritual seeker, with no real concept of what 'consciousness' is. I now live as, in, and through consciousness every second of the day. I thank Saniel and all the others in this work who constantly give me the encouragement and unconditional love I need to speak and live my highest truth with deep integrity."
Maria Balogh, 28, temporary worker

"I met Saniel three years ago and found an instant, profound connection with him, his words, and his transmission. This started an amazing transformational journey, leading to realization of my divine nature and my own teaching and transmission work. Now I am going through the transition from knowing myself as Consciousness alive to owning my divine nature as a Goddess-woman. This is coming through a tremendous, ongoing plunge into and then burning through the depths of my pre-existing life patterns and psychic conditioning. I am deeply grateful to Saniel for what he has brought to us all."
Linda Groves, 44, teacher, photo stylist, production coordinator

"Saniel has offered me so much through his writings, teaching, and transmission that my life has been forever transformed. His groundbreaking work has allowed me to rest in full acceptance of who I am. My seeking has ended, and I now abide as embodied consciousness."
JoAnn Lovascio, 43, healer, teacher, caterer, mother

"For 23 years, I sought my infinite nature as a teacher and practitioner of Transcendental Meditation. Finally, I had to force myself to admit that my awakening might never dawn through that path. Saniel Bonder's writings and presence gave me the information, support, and permission I needed to allow myself to sink into the confusion and separateness he calls 'the core wound.' Soon thereafter, I realized my total Self – both limitless and utterly mortal. Saniel's revolutionary teachings about the core wound, the hypermasculine impulse, and mutuality open the doorway to Self-realization for anyone who seriously seeks it."
Ted Strauss, 43, inventor, educator, seminar leader

"I am a Native American recovering from both substance abuse and religious fundamentalism. I'm also a rape victim and a mother who gave her first two children up for adoption in her teens. Waking Down with Saniel's help is taking me into every broken place and shadow within myself to see, be, and embrace all that I am. When I first heard Saniel speak of the core wound, it was a language I understood. I felt like I had been holding my breath my whole life, and now I could finally breathe. So I know what it is to be a broken, shattered soul. And I now know that this book and Saniel's work can open a journey of unimaginable healing for your whole being. It's not easy, but it is real."
Fay Marie Fields, 46, healer, counselor, office manager

"I've searched for truth and freedom with mindfulness, Osho, Miracle of Love, and many advaitic teachers (with whose assistance I awakened as consciousness) and I'm grateful to all for their help. Saniel's work is different. He has been instrumental in supporting and daring me to be ALL of who I am, including, and especially, the wounded, vulnerable human being. My body, my feelings, my whole Being has entered into a sacred marriage with and as consciousness. I am profoundly grateful."
Hillary Davis, 41, Jin-Shin Jyutsu practitioner, facilitator

"Saniel Bonder's teachings have rolled out the red carpet, given me license to morph into the divine, stinking human animal that I am. The lethal, marooned parts of myself, like black sheep in a family, have been met. I have fallen into myself, at last, and am fertile and lit."
Shauna Gunderson, 43, writer, publicist, mother of two

WAKING
DOWN

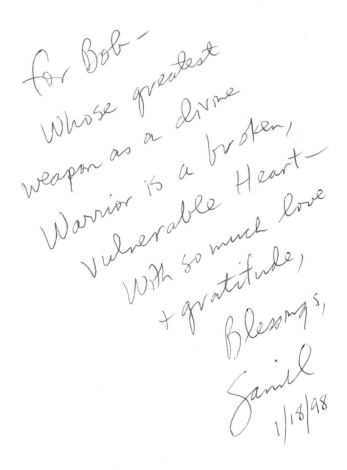

For Bob —
whose greatest
weapon as a divine
Warrior is a broken,
vulnerable Heart —
With so much love
+ gratitude,
Blessings,
Saniel
1/18/98

Shown on the back cover, the logo of the White-Hot Way of Mutuality, also called the Way of Waking Down, is a "yantra" or sacred geometric form designed by Saniel Bonder. The square represents matter, the Earth, and the phenomenal cosmos, physical and psychic. The circle represents consciousness and the transcendent spirit or Sun of Being. The three peaks of Mt. Tamalpais stand for three dimensions of our total identity and relatedness: the infinite consciousness, the psychic soul-nature, and the material, genetic persona, and their corresponding relations. The triangle of conscious spirit drives down into the fathomless Heart-ground of Being – analogous to the source of the human heartbeat. From that ground springs the rose of divinely human realization of Being. Glorious and fragrant, it still has thorns.

Each of Saniel's teaching books will display a portion of this logo as a distinguishing design motif. *Waking Down* is a summary book of essential teachings. For this book, Saniel chose the downward pointing triangle and just the stem of the emerging rose of divinely human Being.

These symbolize essential elements of his White-Hot Way of Mutuality.

This logo is also the trademark of Mt. Tam Awakenings, Inc.

Beyond
Hypermasculine Dharmas

WAKING DOWN

A Breakthrough Way of
Self-Realization
in the Sanctuary of Mutuality

by Saniel Bonder

Mt. Tam Awakenings, Inc.

Library of Congress Cataloging-in-Publication Data

Bonder, Saniel
Waking down: beyond hypermasculine dharmas – a breakthrough way of self-realization in the sanctuary of mutuality
Saniel Bonder. — 1st ed.

ISBN 0-9662304-0-X
Saniel Bonder — Spirituality/Psychology

Mt. Tam Awakenings, Inc., San Anselmo, California

Printed in the United States of America

2 4 6 8 9 7 5 3

FIRST EDITION

Cover design by Daniella Woolf
Cover photograph by Linda Groves
This book is set in Palatino type
and was printed by Rose Printing Co.,
Tallahassee, Florida.

for the Hungry

Also by Saniel Bonder

The White-Hot Yoga of the Heart: Divinely Human Self-Realization and Sacred Marriage – A Breakthrough Way for "Westerners"

The Perpetual Cosmic Out-of-Court Payoff Machine: Selected Essays on the White-Hot Way of Mutuality

While Jesus Weeps: Conversations in the Garden of Gethsemane (a novel)

Contents

Foreword

Say Howdy is an expression of the old West. Born in San Francisco in December 1941, raised in the Central San Joaquin Valley in California, I am a western sort of gal. I grew up surrounded by those values and concepts that were so popular in Hollywood westerns. At first glance, I am hardly a candidate for esoteric Eastern philosophy, and yet I recognized in the heroes and philosophies of Buddhism and Hinduism the similarities to the cowboy and cowgirl heroes of my youth (don't forget that Dale Evans had her own horse, gun, sense of adventure and she wrote the song). Dale Evans was my first glimpse of a tantric goddess long before I ever knew what a tantric goddess was.

In the early 1980s, after years of "do-it-yourself" Buddhist study, I joined a group of Buddhist practitioners and began to seriously and with devotion study and practice the disciplines of that philosophy. During all of those years, it never once occurred to me that I could expect to become realized-awakened-enlightened in this lifetime. This was due to my understanding of personal karma. In an early meditation I had seen my karma; it was an inverted mountain, equivalent to the La Brea Tar Pits. It was huge, dark, oozing, sticky, rank smelling and able to swallow anything that touched it. A type of "original sin." My perception was this: even if I practiced diligently and lived as a good person, helping others and forever striving to be better than I knew how to be, all of the time left to me in this lifetime could not begin to remove that dark mountain. I accepted that. After all, it was true for all humans. I believed it was worth the effort so that future lifetimes would be experienced with less dark karma.

In the mid 1990s, my life began to disintegrate. No part of it was left untouched during this time of loss and destruction. There was nothing I could do to stop it. No matter how I meditated and prayed, no matter what I did, no matter what I didn't do, things got worse. It was agony. Yet as a Buddhist I was told, "How lucky you are! You are paying back your karmic debt big time with such suffering!" I kept on paying.

Eventually, I could no longer work up the interest to do my practice, to meditate, to pray, to live, to die or plain old give a damn. Numbness replaced passion. There was no struggle left in me, no liveliness either. I was in a state of humiliated resignation. I figured I would live out the rest of my life in that condition. I thought that for the first time I would fit right in.

It was at this time in my life that I came into contact with Saniel Bonder and his teaching. Now don't be thinking, "Well sure, this gal was so beaten down that anything would look good to her if it offered to relieve the pain she was in." One of the first things I heard from Saniel was that struggling to escape the pain of your existence maintains the pain of your existence. I remember my mind shrieking, "Oh, no!", and at the same time feeling my body relax for the first time in three years. I had always been taught, and firmly believed, that my mind could get me out of anything if I worked hard enough and thought about it long enough. In an instant, I knew that was a lie. I was where I was and in the state I was exactly because I had followed my mind. I decided to stay and be with that relaxation in my body. Within twenty-four hours, that "relaxation" had turned into a state of dizziness. I was unable to drive, to move quickly or in any way physically distract myself from being exactly who and where I was. My carefully constructed and managed semblance of balance was unraveling, fast!

This appetizer/teaser of a book is meant to stimulate your curiosity and whet your appetite. Buckle up, reader, this ride is not anything like you think it is going to be. It is beyond the rational mind. Be warned that this teaching is alive, messy, juicy, tantric, paradoxical, sacred, human, divine, limited, limitless, and above all: REAL!!!!! It takes you to that very place within your own human-being that you have done everything all of your life to avoid. It is to become that broken/healed heart. From that being-ness you can live, fully liberated and alive, awake in this lifetime.

The teachings of Saniel Bonder are exquisitely original. Many people who have for years sought awakenings through a variety of rigorous practices are awakening with little resistance after reading his first book, *The White-Hot Yoga of the Heart,* and receiving his personal transmission of Being-force. People with little or no past practice are also awakening. Saniel has said that if one reads his writings, attends his transmission sittings and participates with others in this Way of Mutuality, in most cases awakening will occur within two or three years. It is almost guaranteed! As far as I am concerned, realization is a done deal if one follows those simple suggestions. There is no entrance exam other than your heart's desire to be free and awake.

Here's where our gal of the west reappears; she asks about this ability to help others awaken. "Yeah, so what's the point? Do you become awakened to enjoy better sex, to have a better career, to be more and get more? What's the payoff?" Of course, there is no payoff or payout in the usual meaning. What there is is this: a community (sangha for those comfortable with the word) of folks who are committed to living with one another in and from a place called mutuality, no matter what their stage of development and realization.

What is mutuality? Why, it's the real prize! Read on.

Everyone is invited to this grand event. I have lived my life seeking/waiting for this. A way to live with myself and others that allows, in fact encourages, each and every one of us to show up exactly as who we are, with all of our parts present and accountable. Mutuality is not equality, although egalitarianism is a part of it. It is not unity of purpose, although unity is a part of it. It is knowing, at the cellular-molecular level, that there is no difference between you and me. The body relaxes. Although we show up in apparent separation, your right or purpose in being here is as real as my right and purpose in being. It is not a social-political "good idea" or high falutin' principle. It is my body's imperative to live with other bodies in/from a place of mutual recognition, holding and celebration. We are responsible and accountable to ourselves and to each other in equal measure. Each body is completely accountable to the consciousness we embody. Consciousness submits to the body, it is all happening in the livingness of mutuality. My heart is my skin, consciousness is my skin, as I submit to you in mutuality, and we touch, there is a moment of critical mass, infinite alive-ness. Dancing through time and space as the divine and the human in mutuality. Do you wanna dance with me?

This is what I tip my hat to and say "Howdy"!

You'll have to read the book to find out more. I urge you not to limit yourself with a mind that would keep you ignorant in order to defend old ideas. This teaching feels to me as if I were living inside a Bach concerto. It starts out a little precise and measured, doing homage to that which has come before. Just about the time the first yawn is coming (it will be the last!), suddenly the tempo changes and the music roars and the windows fly open and a clean wind comes blasting through, taking away with it all the dust, the old ideas, the stale air of what "was."

Saniel has written, "Awaken and be Who you are. Live the great sacred Dance of Being, the divinely human sacred Marriage, as you are so moved, in tangible intimacy with those most dear to you."

Read on and if you are so moved by the words and what you feel, come and meet us. You will be welcomed.

Until then, happy trails to you.

Susan Sevilla
Santa Cruz, California
November, 1997

Introduction

What if It's Possible to Make Realization Popular?

I appreciate Susan Sevilla's Foreword for many reasons – not least of which is, it's so juicy. This Way of Waking Down that I have in some ways stumbled into revealing is alive, it's cooking, it's like a hothouse plant. It is itself evolving and changing as I write and as you read. Nobody owns it. Everybody should have access to it. As its originator, its pioneer revealer, I have a custodial responsibility to make sure that I have made it as clearly available to you and every other body as possible.

This book provides an introductory, definitive overview. Susan calls *Waking Down* a "teaser" of a book, and she's right. In this goofy age of virtual everything and real nothing, I am a champion of the reality of the body and the reality of relatedness. I'm also a champion of your opportunity to realize who you are as infinite consciousness. "Real-ize." To make real. In some sense, this path of Waking Down does just that. It makes both the living consciousness and the living body real, and real to one another, and real, paradoxically enough, *as* one another. Indeed, Waking Down makes the living consciousness and each and *all* the living bodies real, and real to one another, and real, even more paradoxically, *as* one another. And it exalts, yet does not make a fetish of, the living psyche, including every part of us that has been suppressed, devalued, marginalized, made wrong, condemned, vilified, and betrayed – whether by ourselves or by others.

Recently I read somewhere that one of the Eastern dharmas, or teachings, is making meditation popular in America. But meditation is just a means to an end. It's supposed to lead to awakening, liberation, Self-realization.

My work is an attempt to make *realization* popular in America – and everywhere. Not a hypermasculine or dissociative transcendence of all our messy, human pain and mortality, but a whole being integration of transcendent consciousness and finite matter, eternal spirit and mortal flesh, all our light and all our shadow. This realization is not an end point in evolution, but a whole new life, your second birth.

My friends and I have observed that those who are hungry gravitate naturally, and quite swiftly, into this embodied freedom. Our awakening and awakened bodies make our gathering an alchemical sanctuary – both a womb and a cauldron – of mutuality. We call the process Waking Down. This book is a summary overview, and a White-Hot transmission, of that evolutionary event. Find out for yourself!

You've no doubt noticed that I use a number of words and phrases in distinctive ways. This points to another reason for the present book. In the course of my explorations to articulate this White-Hot Way of Mutuality for others, I have had to come up with a new vocabulary. There is no other languaging of the process of spiritual and conscious growth that even comes close to saying what I am trying to say.

But you know how it is with innovating. If the innovators aren't careful, the new approach winds up working against itself. Even its own terminology becomes arcane and often forbidding to the uninitiated. It appears to me that I now have a complete, self-consistent, and seminal communication to make to you. Therefore, it is my obligation, I feel, to offer to you a single, essential summary of that total communication.

That is the particular task of this book. Each essay provides the best attempt I can make to summarize one or more key elements of my work. These crystallizations will, hopefully, help you get what this Way is about and how it differs from other paths with which you may be familiar. Taken together, these short essays provide a definitive overview of this whole approach to being and becoming.

Though I have devoted my entire adult life to sacred work and have a lively, dramatic story of personal transformation to tell, the purpose of this book is to make a breakthrough way of Self-realization available to *you*. Because others are already joining me in adept service to participants, my personal story is only of secondary value to anyone. The greater communication of our work does not now require it.

For this reason, I have not chosen to make an extensive autobiographical presentation in this first publication of my teachings. For the same reason I do not speak much in this book about the various teachers and gurus who have served me. Of these, two have been by far the most helpful.

The first was the famous modern Hindu sage Ramana Maharshi, whom I never met physically, as he died before my birth. By identifying the place in the physical heart organ that is the seat or locus of divine Self-consciousness, Ramana opened the way for bodily realization of Being as no earlier adept ever had. His living transmission and recorded wisdom revealed the Self in my own heart and established me in my mature exploration of consciousness. But his traditional Indian teachings did not address all the parts of my being that I needed to integrate, and ultimately I had to look elsewhere for help.

The second, and most important, of my gurus was the American-born master named Adi Da (formerly Da Free John). I spent nearly two decades in Adi Da's community, wrote a full-length biography of him, and was, during much of that time, a principal editor for his publications and speaker for his mission. His initiatory revelations of absolute Brightness, his blessings, and his instruction helped enormously to make my awakening and my work possible. I will always be grateful to him, and in many ways I will always love and revere him.

Yet at last, I found his approach wanting. Indeed, it was the crisis of taking my leave from this great guru that empowered my rapid awakening and led to my own work as a teacher-transmitter of our integrity and freedom.

Thus, neither Adi Da nor any other adept or teaching is the source of my realization, or of my work. The White-Hot Way of Mutuality is made as much out of my disaffection with his and other traditional teachers' views of the ultimate process of transformation and their styles of serving disciples, as it is made of what I have positively brought forward from my study and work with them. I try to make honorable acknowledgments where I feel they are appropriate. But if this Way stands in a lineage, it is only the continuously evolving lineage of freedom, love, and trust of Being that transcends all doctrines and traditions.

This book's Epilogue, "The Fire of the Onlyness of Conscious Life," is an anthem to such freedom. It's one of the first full essays I wrote as an adept, in the spring of 1995.

A brief essay at the end of the book provides what its title proclaims: "Some Final Statements on My Life and Work, and Where I Take My Stand."

The book closes with an informative section on "What to Do Next if You Are Interested."

I hope *Waking Down* speaks to your heart and your whole being. If this book does strike a deep resonance in you, I stand ready, along with others, to be of service to you.

May everyone everywhere fall into the incomparable wellness of divinely human embodiment. May everyone everywhere, in his or her own style, choose to live in an authentic sanctuary of mutuality. May each of us, one by one and all together, inherit the conscious magic of Waking Down, so that our species reveals the miracle of That which only human beings can Be and Do.

May this be so for YOU.

Prologue

Breaking the Encryption of Fundamental Human Confusion and Separateness

As a champion of conscious embodiment in relatedness, I am definitely not trying to come up with a process that carries even a whiff of "do-it-yourself-on-your-own." The approach described in this book requires actual, personal connectedness, relatedness face to face. Therefore, I have written this book as something between a menu and an appetizer. If you want the feast in full, you will have to arrange to come and find me, or one or more of my friends who has become, with my help, an autonomous adept of this Waking Down. This approach drives into a deeply grounded cellular transformation of your whole being. I also call it the White-Hot Way of Mutuality. There is no substitute in it for personal connectedness with one or more living adepts, or awakened teacher-transmitters, of that very transformation.

Indeed, though I have been living, transmitting, and teaching this process for nearly five years now, I have never been at liberty to try to manage it on any kind of mass scale. It requires direct, intimate contact and access. If you are going to Wake Down all the way into the ecstatic murk of conscious embodiment, you are going to need qualified help at the ready.

Moreover, you are not only going to need an adept who is personally committed to your awakening and ongoing transformation. You are also going to need true friends who are fellow journeyers on the path. "Mutuality," hm? Relatedness. Immediate, vulnerable, in your life – the Internet and e-mail just won't do. Even the telephone is no complete substitute. The bodily senses and the feeling heart must have the feast of real encounter with others who are complete or certainly maturing templates of the very same freedom and joy that you aspire to.

You also have to be met and held in your subconscious and unconscious depths. You have to be allowed to sink into and integrate all the dark, difficult zones and patterns of who you are that you have always found it necessary to suppress or escape. Being aware together there, speaking to one another in and from these hidden depths of shame and worthlessness – these kinds of contact are every bit as transformative as mutual bodily delight in the obviousness of spirit and consciousness. So I, for one, am not interested in making any communication that Waking Down is possible for those who would deprive their bodily senses and heart of the meal of such communion.

That feast awaits all those who have begun to despair of what I call, in this book's subtitle and throughout the text, "hypermasculine dharmas." I suggest that the force of hypermasculinity is deeply entrenched in all of us and is a primary obstacle to our true wellness of Being. The term hypermasculine includes, but also goes beyond, what people mean nowadays when they speak critically of things patriarchal.

Dharmas are expressions of the fundamental laws and truths that govern our existence. Hypermasculine points to every kind of reactive, dissociative, self-divided, idealistic, or conceptually based stance we human beings chronically take in the midst of our bewildering lives. It also refers to every kind of formulaic, superimposed, aggressive alteration of self, others, and world that we conceive and attempt to execute in order to achieve harmony, happiness, or fulfillment of any and all kinds. Thus, every meditation technique, every psychological and physical regimen for well-being, comes under this umbrella of hypermasculine dharma. You'll have to read on, and then go on to realize what I mean profoundly, before the full extent and impact of our chronic hypermasculinity – even among feminists, Goddess-invokers and -worshippers, and the like – reveals itself to you.

I am not asking you to believe what I am saying. I don't want you to just take it at face value. I am asking you to investigate human culture and your own patterning so thoroughly that what I am saying here either proves itself to you beyond doubt, or not. I am convinced that if we were to conduct that exploration together to our mutual satisfaction, you too would begin to see that all the dharmas – the sustaining truths, belief systems, ideologies, paths, laws, and teachings – of our species to date are hypermasculine. Either they always were, or else they've become so over time.

How is the way of Waking Down different? It's a complete relaxation into the very aspects of Being that hypermasculinity reacts to. It's a falling, a yielding into such a deep acceptance of things as they are that the deeper reality of all that IS reveals itself – and thus prompts the spontaneous transformation of things as they have been. It is a feast of real arrival into and as who you are, in real encounter with others who are doing the same.

This occurs through impassioned cooperation with the mysterious divine grace of the Being-force bestowed by the adepts of this Waking Down. That conscious power of Being grants each and every body an integrity unprecedented in his or her previous experience.

To live this exploration together, while enjoying such a banquet, the ultimate reality of Being, is what I mean by mutuality. In mutuality you become vulnerably accountable to others who, like yourself, are committed to the love, investigation, and expression of true and total Being. And you discover that the matrix of those real relationships becomes an alchemical sanctuary of this superactivated or White-Hot process of transformation. No effort is needed. It just happens. What you have to do to benefit – but it's a lot! – is cooperate, much as a white-water kayaker has to paddle to stay afloat. Its current consumes you. But "it" is YOU.

What makes this Way of Mutuality White-Hot? Expose yourself to it. Let your heart and whole being be touched. You'll find out.

The Being-force that makes all this not only possible but actual did not fall out of the sky. Nor did its precise formulation, as you encounter it here, come from any lineage guru, any deity, any tradition. I have spontaneously manifested it bodily since my own awakening in 1992, and I have greatly refined its transmission and expression during the years since.

As long as I was the only one who could help people into this awakened life, I could not afford to make it available in a public way. The laws of the process required that I devote myself to the small number of people whom I could personally serve on a regular basis. Only such concentrated service could ensure them the best opportunity to awaken. I had to be there for them and with them all the way into and beyond the advent of non-separate freedom.

Now, however, at least ten of my friends have entered what I call the second birth, or divinely human realization of Being, to such a degree that they see they must begin their own awakened service as adepts. Several already have. They are finding such work necessary even for their own growth. Transmitting or radiating this embodied freedom to others has become their spontaneous, effortless reality, and teaching it has become their unavoidable necessity. Another ten or so are awake, and many of them are also moving in the direction of necessary, inevitable adept service.

The Way of Waking Down is structured to grow by the networking that we find natural. Suddenly, I have a network of active or emerging teacher-transmitters. And we and several dozen others who are steadily awakening have found ourselves living in an ever more catalytic alchemy of mutuality. This has occurred without our imposing on ourselves the necessity to create any kind of intentional community. It's a free, natural, voluntary association, which each one chooses or not as he or she is so moved.

So this Way is now ready to grow into much more visible availability in the world at large. It will take this whole book, and many others, for us to even begin to communicate our excitement about it.

What's the essence of that excitement?

We feel we have broken the encryption of fundamental human confusion and separateness.

We sense that we have punched in the access code for a wholesale transformation of human life and culture – in a truly democratic, voluntary, natural manner.

The evidence is continuing to appear in our lives, and those of others, every day. After all the failure, all the despair, all the numb hopelessness, all the endless passages into cul-de-sacs, all the searches that only accomplished cosmetic growth and modest but superficial transformation – we are arriving into a liberated realization that is as human as it is divine, and in which the absolute conscious freedom is as obvious as our fingers and toes, our fears and desires.

We invite you to explore our approach, question it and us to your heart's content, and join us if you wish. No one, no single body, owns this way. Every body manifests his, her, its unique expression. Conscious mutuality requires, and also makes inevitable, democratic gatherings of awakening and awakened beings. Such beings revel in the spontaneous consummation of the marriage of consciousness and matter in every body, and in the worlds wherein these body-forms appear. Together they prompt, I sense, some kind of superintensifying transformation of everything and everyone.

Again: White-Hot.

One

Waking Down

For thousands of years, some of humanity's most creative and inspired men and women have been dedicating themselves to one or another kind of attempt to wake up. This is particularly true of religious enthusiasts and spiritual seekers. Such people are always trying to wake up.

The White-Hot Way of Mutuality certainly produces powerful awakenings. Some of those who practice it find that, at least for a time or periods of time, it catalyzes spiritual ascent. Their energies rise. Subtle centers in or associated with the head open and come alive. So this Way is not opposed to waking up in any number of forms.

It's just that the fundamental thrust or drive of this process takes you down. Thus, the whole evolutionary event I am facilitating, at both the individual and collective levels, can be summarized as "Waking Down."

There are two principal forms of this descent. They usually accompany, parallel, and further catalyze one another.

First, you discover or find your own conscious nature. You do so by falling out of identification with the thinking and even the intuitive or perceptual mind, and into identification with the conscious Heart of your whole being. You see that you have become situated in the conscious ground of Being.

The second form of descent may to some degree precede the first. In it your fundamental energy of life and mind, or psyche, falls ever more deeply into embodiment.

Thus, as one of my friends described it, you fall into your conscious identity and your physical body at the same time – more or less. In ways that you never have before.

Waking Down is landing in your own real existence, not just as infinite consciousness but as a finite human being. It's an arriving into your own life. You really can't appreciate it until it happens. Indeed, you may be sitting here reading these words and thinking,

"Right. Exactly! I know about this. This is what has happened to me."
Maybe.

If you want to look into it together – we'll have to see over time, hm?

I am not trying to pull rank or put anyone down. I am simply offering you the benefit of many years of living and teaching. Many people have come thinking that what I am talking about has already taken place for them. I have never once been so pleasantly surprised. I'm not saying it can't happen. I'm just saying, we'll have to see.

In these pages we will have plenty of opportunities to contemplate other kinds of realization of consciousness and other kinds of spiritual or psychological descent. It is important for me to draw at least some initial distinctions between these and what I mean by Waking Down.

One significant distinction is that, in Waking Down, the conscious nature – that aspect of who and what you are that is simply aware of your field of existence and experience – does not dis-identify with your body, mind, and individual personality in order to enforce an exclusive identification with itself.

Some teachers and teachings assert that this is the only way to realize consciousness. They say you have to rigorously sift out the conscious principle by discovering how it is absolutely not those things: "I am not the body. I am not this desire. I am not that thought. I am not sensation. I have no relationships. I have no form. I have no color. I am consciousness only, free of everything and everyone that comes and goes, even free of this body that is only going to die anyway!"

The realization of conscious freedom in Waking Down certainly anchors you in and as that absolute, untouchable nature of Being. But in doing so it does not require you in effect to uproot or do violence to all the rest of who and what you are. Rather, the conscious nature comprehends that it is at once completely free *of* all the other components of the whole human being, and free *as* them.

This is an extremely subtle paradox, but it becomes very real for you as this awakening unfolds. The new form of comprehension occurs through bodily realization rather than mere thinking or affirmation. The knowing that arises is a whole being-feeling-knowing. It's not an ideation, nor even a subtle intuition based in the higher mind.

Another important distinction between this and other approaches: nowadays, many teachers and teachings are preaching acceptance of the dark side of our nature, the shadow psyche of subconscious and unconscious impulses. They and others also counsel an integration of spirit and matter, offering techniques for how to contact limitless spirit and then bring it into the body.

As you will see if you find yourself deeply attracted to this White-Hot Way of Mutuality, those forms of acceptance and integration are still somehow doing violence. They are reinforcing splits in our total being even while counseling all kinds of methods for achieving integration. They are subtly struggling against even that which they would urge us to accept.

How so? In physics it is understood that every action engenders an equal and opposite reaction. The same is true in the realm of psychic activity. Thus, methodical techniques attempt to enforce qualities of acceptance and integration upon the living human organism. To the degree the action is forced, it sabotages its very intention. And meanwhile, at a deeper psychic level, the individual is still struggling against – and thereby, in a subtle way, at once sustaining and reacting to – the motivating stress of his or her non-acceptance and non-integration.

The currents of action and reaction thus engendered weaken the intention and compromise the results of one's action. Outcome: you're trying to relax, and you sort of do relax. But if you can sense a deeper current of your reality, you also feel underneath that you are even more tense. You feel that something is vaguely but even more wrong than before.

This path of Waking Down accomplishes a thorough integration of consciousness, body, psyche or mind, and soul or spirit. How? The transmission of awakening Being-force activates your core feeling-conscious nature at the very heart of your bodily existence. Gradually you begin to notice that you are thinking, feeling, and acting from a different depth, a ground, a feeling of freedom even in the midst of all your shadow stuff.

Meanwhile, your adept friends and others welcome you to just be as you are from day to day, however that may look or feel. You show up feeling like scum of the earth, with all your worst junk hanging out. They get you to say a few words about it – and suddenly they are cheering you on and praising you. And you are invited, especially at the beginning, to *do* as little as possible about, or in relation to, anything. You are invited not to opt for your trusty hypermasculine toolkit of self-reassuring techniques. Instead, people will say, "Keep willful effort to a minimum. Just come around, hang out, expose yourself to the transmission. Read Saniel's writings, talk about how it feels. You'll see."

Outcome: however long it takes, you eventually see that you can't help but accept and be more and more of your true and total Self. You just keep on becoming more and more the precise, crystalline event that you are, all at once, infinite and finite, divine and human, unmanifest and ever so concrete.

As that endless becoming proceeds, all of your previous beliefs about reality get challenged, and you wind up leaving many of them in your wake.

Most spiritual paths counsel us to take up intentional disciplines to change and improve, even to perfect, our bodies, minds, and souls. Only thus, it is said by some, can we ever hope to awaken to and as That which absolutely transcends the body, mind, and soul.

This approach, in contrast, urges you from the outset to do as little as you possibly can to alter and improve body, mind, and soul. It proposes you do absolutely nothing to perfect any part of yourself. And it challenges the very notion that you even can do such a thing, really.

Many teachings hold that humanity has fallen from some primordial divine state of grace and must now seek redemption.

This teaching suggests that humanity is simply the cutting edge of cosmic evolution. It argues that those who live in human form are doing the most daring work in Being to attempt the fullest integration of all that IS.

Most teachings hold that there is something fundamentally wrong with every human being, something that must be fixed.

This teaching proposes that there is absolutely nothing wrong with any human being, even the most heinous or deluded. It does not therefore suggest that murder, mayhem, and insanity are OK in human society. No, it simply suggests that all imbalances and dislocations from our true and total reality – which includes each and all others as well as our own selves – must be, and also can be, healed most fully by our whole-body realization of Being and our active commitment to real mutuality. And it holds that this can be done and is now being done by ordinary men and women.

Most religions and spiritual teachings point to a liberation from this life and this world, or else a blessed acceptance of this life within this world.

This teaching points to a liberation *into* this life and this world. It prophesies a liberation of so divine a nature, and of such a collective authenticity, that over evolutionary time not only human life but even this and all other manifest worlds will be radically transformed by our liberated presence and spontaneously blessed action within them. Thus, this Way signals an ultimate liberation *of* the world, not merely *from* it.

I could go on and on. The point I am trying to suggest here is that as you come into conscious embodiment through Waking Down, your whole view of the world, and of human history and culture, is likely to go through wholesale shifts and shatterings. I expect you may encounter some of those whitewater rapids of the mind as you read this very book. I know you will encounter many of them if you do find it necessary to Wake Down with my friends and me.

Is "know" too strong a word? Let's just say experience prompts me to state it strongly. I will certainly admit it if I am proved wrong.

I have a suspicion that those who Wake Down together with my friends and me are going to see, more and more, that the whole view of reality we even could have had before Waking Down was dreadfully inadequate and distorted.

I predict that a tremendous new force in human society is emerging in and as this sacred culture of those who Wake Down into White-Hot, conscious mutuality.

I feel great numbers of human beings, human *bodies*, getting ready to relax their endless, anxious searches and fall into deep and total Self-acceptance.

As this occurs, I anticipate that those of us who do this soon, and the many more to come, will someday look back at the entire saga of human history that has preceded us. And we will marvel at how uptight and out of touch with living, physical, fleshy, and relational reality the whole human race used to be – even its most apparently worldly hedonists and materialists, as well as its great spiritual masters, mystics, and sages.

But let's not get caught up in my premonitions and predictions. Let's get into the heart of this matter for *you*.

Two

The Onlyness

M ost of the key terms and phrases that I use in my
work are of my own coinage. "Onlyness" is one of
the few that I have derived from the usage of others.
My adept-teacher Adi Da used to say to his early students,
"There is *only* God." He clarified that he was not just saying that
there is God. Mystics, saints, and yogis had said such a thing since
ancient times, he noted. Adi Da indicated that they were pointing
thereby to some overarching divine reality that is different from our
ordinary, mundane reality. The "God" or divine truth to which they
pointed perhaps encompasses and pervades but is nonetheless, even
if only in some extremely subtle way, separate or distinct from the
ordinary reality we experience every day.

That is not the kind of God or divine truth to which he himself
was pointing. The great reality, he said, is not just existing as an
alternative to what we already know and experience. It is also *being*
all of that even while including more transcendent and invisible
dimensions and qualities. The great reality, he said, is *only*. "There is
only God."

I had temporary, partial intuitions of this *only* reality during
my many years with my teacher. Nonetheless, it was not until I
relinquished my discipleship and devotion to him and my practice
of his teaching that I was able to come into my own, self-validating
realization of this great principle.

For a number of reasons, I do not find it useful to speak of
"God." Instead, I simply refer to that great principle of All-Being as
"the Onlyness" – with a capital "O."

One of the things I really like about this phrase is that it
contains no numbering. Mystics, saints, yogis, and other teachers or
enlightened individuals often speak of "Oneness." Indeed, "yoga"
– from the same root as "yoke" – is traditionally understood as
action that produces the realization of union, unity: Oneness. Seekers and New Age enthusiasts are full of the language of Oneness.

More discriminating sages, and certainly many intellectual seekers, prefer to avoid the potentially theistic or entity-presuming implications of such ways of pointing to the great reality. They often speak, instead, of that reality as "non-dual." You can't exactly describe It as "One," they say; but you can point to It as That which is "not *two*."

When you arrive in conscious embodiment, I suggest, manifest phenomena and events no longer appear any less real or divine than unmanifest ones. The fact that they are temporal and subject to change only indicates qualities that distinguish them from those components of reality that are eternal and never subject to change. These qualities do not, however, make them less divine, or less real. Not in my view, or according to my definitions of these terms.

Therefore, I sense that most of those who point to the "non-dual" reality are actually making a most subtle distinction between what they regard to be that ultimate non-dual reality and the world of dualities and multiplicities that we constantly encounter in ordinary living.

So I talk about the Onlyness. And I also refer to It as the "Non-Dual Multiplicity." There is no all-encompassing distinction between that reality and ordinary reality. It IS ordinary reality, as well as all extraordinary reality. It just IS, period. It is all consciousness, all spirit, all energy, all form, all matter, all beings, worlds, and events. It just IS That which IS.

Some schools and teachings make much of "emptiness." They would perhaps take issue with these statements here as being "substantialist" – presuming or affirming that there is some great substance, principle, or being that is the actual root and essence of reality.

I don't think so. I hold as follows: the conscious principle that is to be realized as absolutely non-different from all forms and substances is not, in and of itself, any kind of substance. It is no discrete being of any kind, nor even an infinite Being that has some kind of substantial reality which we can posit to be in any way, shape, or form apart from or other than absolute non-objectivity or non-substantiality. Any entity, anything possessing any substance at all, must therefore be to some degree an objective phenomenon.

The conscious principle, then, is a paradox. It is realized, ultimately, to be perfectly subjective and yet perfectly non-separate from any and all objective phenomena. To one who enjoys this realization, its emptiness, then, is no more compelling than its fullness.

Such is the Onlyness – the Non-Dual Multiplicity.

I expect some readers may be getting nervous. No, I am not going into endless hair-splitting about such matters. It is just necessary to establish a few points about the philosophical stand that I take. Over the course of this book I will have other such occasions.

But this teaching, in any case, is not speculative or intellectual philosophy. Those who are looking for such will find it wanting.

That's fine with me. I find *them* wanting. That's why this book, like all my others, is dedicated first and foremost to "the Hungry." The Hungry with a capital "H" cannot abide living without utterly embodied realization of the Onlyness with a capital "O." They eat living words of inspiration for breakfast, lunch, and dinner, and all day long, and they spit out mere intellection as if it were poison.

Three

Being = Identity + Relatedness

I have one more series of considerations for you that some readers may find a little abstract, but which, again, I do not intend in any such vein. Get into all this with your whole heart and see if it doesn't provide a transfusion of healthy life-blood.

Another of the terms I use to speak of the great reality is, simply, "Being." For me it's synonymous with "Onlyness." But it's a commonly used word, one that most people can get comfortable with. The very sound of it carries the implication somehow that this is reality in a form that we can really trust, if only we get to know or be it.

As an example of how that might be so, a longtime Buddhist said to me once that, given his training in the inherent self-lessness of reality, it is hard for him to conceive of the ultimate nature or principle as "Self" – whereas, the word "Being" was a lot easier to work with. Many theists can also tolerate "Being" as a designation for the divine, and many non-theists or atheists can handle it as a designation for the Larger Picture, so to speak, if there even is such a thing.

Since I am not trying to get people to hypothesize about anything, but am trying, rather, to help them relax into the completely non-hypothetical existence of whatever IS so for them, I have come to use the term "Being" to denote that IS-ness or AM-ness.

Over the years of my work it has occurred to me that it is quite useful to consider that there are, for our subjective human purposes and aspirations, two great dimensions or qualities in Being. One is identity, or the realm of the self, and the other is relatedness, or the realm of the other. These two, of course, overlap and spill into each other in myriad ways. But we might say that they are, in some senses, the "yin and yang" of Being. Like the Chinese principles of yin and yang, identity and relatedness are the opposite, contrasting, yet interlinked, and always merging or ultimately non-different, two great aspects of the Onlyness that is Being.

Thus, a little equation: "Being = Identity + Relatedness."

Almost every crucial element of the White-Hot Way of Mutuality, including my critical appreciation of other and previous teachings, hinges to a large degree around this definition of Being and its yin and yang of identity and relatedness. This particular distinction provides us enormous leverage in our work to discern how each of us can come into the most complete realization and expression of who we are.

Such realization and expression, you see, cannot be confined to events within the merely subjective field of identity. They must include our realization and expression of Being in the field of relatedness.

Many Oriental teachings exclude the total field of relatedness from fundamental divine reality. They say, to put it bluntly, that the world is unreal. ("The world" is presumed to include all the changing or individuated components of one's own being, such as body, emotions, mind, desires, psyche, and even, for many schools, soul-essence or the sheer feeling of "I"-ness. It also, of course, includes all the components of existence that are external or other to one's own individuated being.)

Many Occidental teachings exclude fundamental divine reality from the specifically human field of identity. *They* say, to put it bluntly, that only the One God is real, and that that God is eternally Other and apart from, or in any case ultimately superior to, even the essence of the individual soul (although possibly permeating and pervading it).

Shankara, a great medieval teacher in India, suggested something that sounds very different. He said, yes, the world is unreal, and yes, only "Brahman" (the Supreme Self) is real. But then he added a paradoxical third proposition: it also must be understood, he said, that "Brahman is the world."

In my teachings, I try to indicate how the White-Hot Way of Mutuality permits the fullest possible realization of all three of those aphoristic statements. I'll also point out ways in which we can be lulled into thinking we are enjoying that fullness of realization when such may not at all be the case.

The work of the most complete realization and expression of both identity and relatedness makes for a most complete participation in reality. And when conscious identity embraces relatedness to the degree that my friends and I have found to be not only possible but even at last an evolutionary necessity – well, I suggest that then, even the infrastructure of Nature begins to be transformed to an extreme degree by our very presence.

Let me see if I can express this more concretely.

The Oriental schools have historically almost cornered the market, we might say, on transcendent Self-realization. But they have tended, in general, to define such realization or awakening in almost entirely subjective terms, pointing exclusively to changes in one's quality of identity. The essence of consciousness, or that principle of our existence which is sheerly just awareness itself, is also the essence of identity.

What I am proposing is that when consciousness is most fully realized, liberated, and expressed, it ceases merely to embody the serenity of transcendent identity or Self. It embraces such an extreme exposure to relatedness, the realm of the Other, that it also finds its identity – its Onlyness – in and as the Other, and every discrete other.

Now, to say that the conscious principle embraces anyone or anything could appear to be speaking about some aspect of mind or psyche that is other than consciousness in itself.

Well, I don't know how to get at this other than to suggest that at some point that conscious principle itself – not just the mind, not just the psyche, not just the individuated soul-essence – embraces such an extreme exposure to relatedness that it not only feels it is being the other. It also, and all the more so, finds itself living in continual responsiveness to the unknowable mystery of the Other. It does so while participating in and as the Onlyness of Self or identity in Being with each and every thing or being that is "Other" in any way or to any degree.

Such is conscious mutuality: the meeting, indeed the wedding, the endless, mad dance and startling, ordinary paradox, of identity and relatedness. What it means in more practical terms is that those who realize such commitment to authentic relatedness, as well as integrated identity, become vulnerable, accountable, accessible participants in real, personal, ordinary human relationships – even with people they are serving as awakened adepts of Being. They cease to presume that their lofty realizations of ultimate identity justify any kind of immunity to the give-and-take of emotional openness to others.

They cannot, then, rationalize what others may feel are such realizers' own insensitivities, issues, and failings. So those realizers stay open to their own human weaknesses and frailties in relationship, their incapacity to know what is the truth of anyone or any-thing, while simultaneously living in the paradox of whole being feeling-realization of the infinite and sublime Onlyness that IS everyone and everything.

This particular point is difficult to reduce to a few words. As this book proceeds, we'll come back to it on a number of occasions. If you come to get to know us, you'll no doubt have opportunities to see other adepts here and me doing our best to put this cornerstone of our work and our way into practical demonstration.

How good we are at it – you'll have to decide for yourself.

Four

The Core Wound of Confusion and Separateness

Until you realize the Onlyness of consciousness and all phenomena, your existence in the realm of identity is one of chronic confusion about who and what you are. And, until such realization, your existence in the realm of relatedness is one of chronic separateness from all things and beings, and even from the Onlyness itself.

Until you awaken, what I call "the core wound" of such chronic confusion and separateness is who and what you *are*. It is not merely something you are experiencing, like birth trauma or a bad dream. It is not just an hallucination which, if only you could see that you are hallucinating, you would stop it. No – such suppositions dishonor the evolutionary plight of the natural human being previous to the realization I teach and offer. Until such clarification of identity, your confusion is *real*. Until such linking up again in ultimate relatedness, your separateness is *real*.

Human beings have a hard enough time acknowledging and permitting these real qualities of, again, not just their experience, but their very nature and existence. We do not need any more shrill, escapist spirituality haranguing us about the sinfulness and even the self-imposed character of our confusion and separateness. The work of outgrowing our bewilderment and pain is difficult in any case. Ideologies that beat us up about all that just add more torment. And they are so fundamentally wrong that they sabotage the very movement into salvation or liberation that they are striving to activate. Those who preach such things are as if throwing imaginary lifelines to a drowning man and then blaming him for not being able to catch hold and be rescued.

You can probably sense that I have developed a certain edge about teachings that make you and me wrong for suffering, or having suffered, our confusion and separateness. I can understand

25

that they were, apparently, the best evolutionary understanding we human beings could muster up till now. But that does not let religion and spirituality off the hook. Billions of men and women, at this very moment, are swallowing their indoctrinations into belief systems that, in one or many ways, make them believe that the very fact of being alive in such confusion and separateness is somehow sin, evil, missing the mark, failing.

Since I have hardly introduced this new understanding yet, I won't go on and on here about the inadequacy of previous understandings. But I must propose to you, if for no other reason than to make you sit up and take close notice, that I am saying something here of tremendous importance. I am confident that the understanding I propose of the fundamental human problem or disturbance is an immense breakthrough in our practical ability to solve the problem, or to heal the disturbance, at the very source. And that, to me, is in turn a most definitive characteristic of any attempt to get at what it is that ails us. If the diagnosis does not in turn lend itself to an eminently practical and practicable cure for anyone who really accepts the diagnosis, then I say there must be something wrong with the diagnosis. It's not the patient's fault if he can't grasp the diagnosis sufficiently to be able to embrace the cure effectively. I say that what ails us is so fundamentally disturbing to everyone that if and when people become available to hear any diagnosis of it, they will promptly apply the medicine and heal themselves once and for all.

I just started that last paragraph by saying I wasn't going to keep on railing about previous attempts to diagnose and treat the fundamental human problem. But then I couldn't help but go and do exactly that. Well, why couldn't I? I suppose it's because I am so sobered by the degree to which every body is held in the maw of judgmental, dissociative philosophies and belief systems.

Let me try again, and I'll see if I can't just get right to the core of your own situation here.

It is absolutely, one hundred percent natural, appropriate, inevitable, and OK for you to be confused about who you are, or whatever is the ultimate Self or identity.

It is absolutely, one hundred per cent natural, appropriate, inevitable, and OK for you to feel separate, most if not all the time, from everyone, everything, even God or whatever you conceive and maybe sometimes have felt to be the ultimate connectedness, or love.

If, in order to Wake Down, you come to me or one of the

adepts who work with me, we are going to spend, I assure you, a lot of time just getting you to relax into your confusion and separateness. We are going to work very hard to help you see that you are really OK just as you are.

There's a paradox here, of course. You can't really accept yourself *as* you are until you have begun to recognize just exactly *what* you are. Yet, as we will discuss more in Chapter Sixteen with regard to what I call "Quantum Vision," the very instant of such recognition also begins to change what, and who, and how you are.

We don't need to dwell on such mysteries at the moment, though. I just want you to take a deep breath and begin to feel into all the ways you have been taught, programmed, conditioned, browbeaten, propagandized, argued, persuaded, and seduced into assuming, deep down and most fundamentally, that there is something very, very wrong with you.

Now, take that a little further. Notice that you are, in fact, confused about who you are. On some level you must be – unless you're just reading this book for confirmation of what you have already realized. But if you have not realized the supreme, infinite, conscious Self-nature of Being, then do you in any way have the feeling that "there must be more than this, what I am already being, who I am"? And if you have realized that infinite identity, then is there in any even infinitesimal way a concern, uneasiness, or discomfort about all the rest of who you are – your personality, your personal soul, your body, your feelings, your shadow reactivity and insecurity, your ethnic identity, your place and responsible obligations in the human world of others?

Most people will be able to admit that there is indeed a fundamental confusion about who they are. One way or another, at one or another end of the spectrum of identity, something is off. Something is unclear.

To continue, then: also notice that you are in reality always tending, chronically, to return to one or another degree of separateness. Sometimes, perhaps even for extended periods, you may enjoy qualities of love, union, communion, connectedness with all things and beings and even the ultimate reality. But, in most cases, there is always a snapping back into a baseline experience of intractable alienation, isolation, cut-offness.

Spiritual seekers are always struggling to achieve some kind of final transcendence of this confusion about who they are and this separateness from all relations. They usually do so by striving to enter and then to maintain sublime states of Self-realization and divine union. They fret and punish themselves when it appears that they have had such a state and then lost it. And most, if not all, their teachings and teachers support that self-deprecating view.

I am suggesting, in contrast, that you give yourself the opportunity to relax deeply into the essential rightness, the evolutionary naturalness, of your confusion and separateness. Let me explain why. This is not just a clever technique for overcoming them, you see. From my perspective, it is rather the only way to do proper homage to who and what we are as human beings.

Until we awaken as the Onlyness, until we realize Being in the manner I am describing, I suggest to you that we *are* the core wound of confusion, in identity, and separateness, in relatedness. This great awakening comprises a total and irrevocable healing of that fundamental confusion and fundamental separateness. But in order for the healing to occur, we must relax our efforts to deny, escape, leap out of, fend off, or penetrate, analyze, and conquer this most primal confusion and separateness at the core of our existence.

Let me tell you why I feel that our confusion and separateness are absolutely natural, inevitable, and appropriate.

It's simply this: we human beings are equal parts infinite and finite.

Our mortal, limited, vulnerable, threatened, finite nature (our bodies, minds, and feelings) never ceases to be obvious to us. Yet, at the same time, there is always the feeling or intuition, "There must be more than this!" If it appears not to be present, others may sense that that particular individual has resigned himself or herself to cynicism or despair. Most people, though, can't help but feel that there must be more to life than what they are already being.

Statistically, very few of the billions of men, women, and children on this planet are intellectually convinced that it is even possible for them to realize a dimension of Being that is infinite, transcendental, eternal, all-pervading, and inexhaustibly free and happy. But most of them yearn, strive, or struggle in one way or another to realize – to make real – more than what is already theirs, or already obvious. Everybody either wants to be more than what he or she is already being, or wishes that he or she could even seriously want such a thing. Almost everybody, anyway.

Similarly, very few of us alive today (or at any time in the past) know or even suspect that it is possible to realize a quality of Love that is universal and indelibly connected, no matter what happens in our lives, or even our deaths. But that doesn't stop people from yearning endlessly for love, connectedness, trust, and the bodily demonstration of it with others. Everybody – or, all right, almost everybody – either wants more love and no separation, or wishes that he or she could even seriously want such a thing.

This chronic squeeze play between what is obviously real and what we sense is potential drives us humans bonkers. It also fuels and drives everything that makes us change and grow. I hear repeatedly about the superior wisdom of all kinds of life forms, from angels to cetaceans. Well, I must confess to being a human chauvinist! It appears to me that we have a built-in evolutionary catalyst that will not allow us to stop at anything less than the fullest integration of infinite conscious spirit and finite, local matter. But, until that integration is fundamentally accomplished, we suffer a crippling wound at the very core of our existence.

I call it the core wound of confusion and separateness. It is not sin. It is not a primordial fall from Grace. It is not evil. It is not the devil's work. It is the preliminary, makeshift, inevitable result of the appearance of a life-form on Earth that is as finite as a stone and as infinite as a god. If we step back and look at this event called human being through the lens of long cosmic time, these several thousand years – maybe, according to some, actually several hundred thousand years – during which humanity has been suffering existence as the core wound, our chronic confusion and separateness is quite understandable. We are having a hard time getting here. We are struggling to clarify our nature. And in the meantime, and in the midst of all our efforts of every kind, there is a great motivating bewilderment, pain, anxiety, craving, yearning, and aspiration: the core wound.

The trick is to go through whatever you must to allow the silent agony/ecstasy of this paradox. You are already both infinite and finite. Short of some kind of transmutation of absolutely everything, at least for the extent of this lifetime you always will be both infinite and finite. And, based on this investigation of our nature, that's likely to be the case even after death, in subtler world zones. But let's not worry about all that for now. We're here in concrete form, and yet we are always driven to something more, or to make the most of it, or to change it, or to transcend it.

In the midst of all that striving, sooner or later you begin to allow yourself to endure the tight squeeze of simultaneity. One of the marvelous mysteries of Waking Down is that, as it turns out, the most sustainable realization of your infinite conscious nature hinges upon your spontaneous capability to permit or accept your finite material and psychic nature. In other words, by allowing and relaxing into your finite, local, human self, with all its limits, frailties, and failings, you avail yourself of the opportunity for the fullest possible realization and expression of your divine nature. And this integration of the two stimulates, remarkably enough, an inexorable, biological process that then, over time, actually heals and transmutes those limited, frail, weak qualities of your true and total Being. In other words, the healing eventuates not as a result of anxious seeking but rather as a result of peaceful, if often quite intense, cooperation with what is already inevitable.

Do you get a sense of the difference? It's like the difference between paddling a canoe upstream against a raging current – good luck, right? – and simply using a paddle to steer while being carried downstream by a current that also sometimes rages, but in any case never stops streaming along.

I'll say more about the core wound in upcoming chapters. This one consideration is the crux of the whole process of Waking Down. If you can grab hold of it and make it your own, you will have slipped through the looking glass into the radiant world of spontaneous initiation, realization, and expression of Who YOU Are.

Five

A Subjective Moebius Strip – The Continuum of Identity (Genetic Nature, Soul-Nature, Transcendent Nature)

H ave you learned somewhere along the line to think of yourself as having a "lower self" and a "higher self"? Or a "soul" that's different somehow from your "ego"? And maybe a "transcendent Self" that is different from both?

I feel that one of the ways we hamstring our capacity to know who we are is by assuming that, somehow, these different parts of our identity are discrete, with distinct boundaries. I suggest that identity is a continuum, stretching, yes, from infinite, non-individuated consciousness all the way through the ranges of archetypal and soul personae into our ordinary, mortal, everyday human ego-selves. It may indeed be true that some individuals while alive, and everyone at death, awakens to a subtler element of who they are and ventures forth in world-zones that differ in many ways from the Earth we know in the waking state. Even so, if we take the long view of human and cosmic evolution, I still feel strongly about this. Identity is a paradoxical continuum. I don't think it is either fruitful or really possible to find out where consciousness stops and the soul-nature begins, or where the soul stops and the ego-self begins.

I've sometimes used a homemade Moebius strip to illustrate this theme. Take a strip of paper. Notice that it has an obvious top and an obvious bottom. Also notice that the top and the bottom are completely distinct from one another. At no point do they intersect or become the same. Now, also notice that the strip of paper has two edges along its length and another two along its width. The opposite edges, similarly, do not intersect at any point.

Now take one end of the strip of paper and turn it one half

twist. Then tape it to the other end so that it smoothly merges.

And, now look again: if you trace your finger along the top, you soon wind up tracing your finger along the bottom, without any apparent dividing line between the two. Similarly, if you trace your finger along one edge lengthwise, you soon wind up tracing your finger along the other edge lengthwise – without any apparent dividing line between the two. Meanwhile, all suggestion of any kind of edge or stopping place along the width has dissolved. The strip of paper is one continuous event, for all intents and purposes, with one surface and one edge only!

So it is, I propose, with the various elements of our human identity. Who and what we are is a paradox, a mystery, and a continuum not unlike a Moebius strip. Various teachers and teachings make what appear to be august pronouncements about these matters as if they were communicating absolute and eternal truth. I don't think so. I think that there are any number of ways we might symbolize the continuum of our identity in words, and some might be more accurate to the totality than others. Even so it is all a rather arbitrary slicing of the Onlyness. It appears to be important to do so in order to help us not only make sense of our experience but, more to the point, to help us realize our existence and express our truths.

Having realized my own true and total nature to the degree that I have, and having examined many secular and sacred traditions' ways of characterizing the different components and aspects of human identity, I speak of three primary nodes on the continuum of our selfhood. At one end, we might say, is the individuated, finite, genetic, psycho-physical persona we have known ourselves to be especially in the waking state in our daily lives on Earth. In the middle, in a sense (and not, in another sense), is the individuated, yet not exactly finite, archetypal and spiritual soul-nature. This portion of us also partakes of the non-individuated or universal soul-nature as well. And at the far end of the continuum, it appears to me, is the non-individuated, infinite, non-personal, transcendental conscious principle, which is both the very essence of All of who we are and the supreme or absolute real nature of All that IS.

I am happy to admit, again, that this is still an arbitrary rendering of our IS-ness. But it has worked for my friends and me, so I use it. It appears to me to possess as much viable, practical accuracy as any other attempt at gauging and naming the parts of human identity.

Here, I'll pass along a key hint for your understanding of how the White-Hot Way of Mutuality works, and why it works so well, for those who find it compelling.

The first great passage in your Waking Down process, in this Way, expedites your most direct integration of the supreme, infinite, non-individuated conscious nature with your individuated, finite, genetic, psycho-physical persona. Once that passage is completed, then the various dimensions of the soul-nature find their way into awakened manifestation or expression. But the soul-nature, or the total expanse of mind and psyche, is in some ways the last to be folded into the integrated, realized life. And, in some ways forever thereafter, the mind, as I have often joked with my friends, is like your dumb kid brother. It never does quite catch up. It's always just coming out of the dark about what you already passed through, consciously and bodily, an hour or a day or a week ago.

Six

The First Birth and Its Now Ending Evolutionary Heyday

hen I was writing my first book of teachings, *The White-Hot Yoga of the Heart*, I included a chapter titled, "The Backbone of This Book." The backbone of that chapter itself is an extensive essay, "The White-Hot Yoga of the Heart and the Three Great Births of Divinely Human Being." I have since chosen "the White-Hot Way of Mutuality" as the principal and preferred designation for this Waking Down process – mostly because I want to highlight the principle of mutuality and avoid unnecessary use of terms that are not English ("yoga") or too easily misinterpreted ("Heart"). Also, I have refined my articulation of my teachings quite a bit since writing that first book, which retains its title, *The White-Hot Yoga of the Heart*.

Nonetheless, that particular essay remains a cornerstone for your understanding of what I am offering you and everyone. It will be included in *The Perpetual Cosmic Out-of-Court Payoff Machine: Selected Essays on the White-Hot Way of Mutuality*. If my transmission and teachings become important for you, I urge you to consider that essay carefully and often over the coming years.

Three great births mark our entire evolutionary history and trajectory, even far beyond our appearance in what we now know to be human life-forms and what we now know to be this universe. In this chapter, I want to define and take a look with you at what I call the first birth of the human being.

The first birth is the quality of human existence that is characterized by the core wound of confusion in identity and separateness in relatedness.

The evolutionary epoch of the first birth, in my view, includes all of human history – at least, till now.

In that longer essay on the three births, I take great pains to indicate why existence in confusion and separateness is the necessary, inevitable, even biologically natural condition for human beings in their first births. I won't try to recapitulate all that here. My argument there has to do with the biology of conception and its relation to the initial merging, in human form, of infinite consciousness and finite bio-matter. Without going into all the anatomical details, I can say here that it appears to me that the union of the sperm and the egg in the first, biological birth – that of the human infant – produces or coincides with a most fundamental dis-ease in the very heart of the infant's being. Neither the conscious nor the material principles ever come to complete clarity in themselves and ease with one another thereafter, until that person's second birth.

Thus, it appears that for perhaps many thousands of years, human beings have suffered fundamental confusion and attenuation of their identities and chronic separateness and limitation in their relatedness.

Now, you might protest that there have always been some in every generation who have overcome this separation and bewilderment. "What about all the mystics, saints, yogis, sages, God-men, avatars, Buddhas, and prophets who have proclaimed realization of Being and freedom from all separateness? What about those who have demonstrated amazing capacity to help others find their own true nature and transcend the sense of separateness while themselves alive? What about all these people? Do they amount to nothing? Were they lying? Were they deluded? Did they somehow misinterpret the phenomena of their own realizations? But if so, how do you explain the incredible, forceful impact they had on others? Or, Saniel, are you just trying to puff yourself up and make grandiose claims for something that, at best, you have only lately begun to share with the historical pioneers of divine unity in many traditions and throughout history?"

These are all good questions. I can't really do justice in this space to what it would, and will, take to answer them in any kind of thorough way. In *Waking Down*, which I have to restrict to providing a definitive overview of the White-Hot Way of Mutuality, I can make only a few initial and provisional points in reply.

First, of course there have been great saints, avatars, mystics, men and women of many distinctive types of enlightenment or liberation, throughout our recorded history as a species. I do acknowledge them and honor their work. But I feel that we would all do well to outgrow our views of religious and spiritual wisdom as static bodies of unquestionable knowledge and belief. We would do far better to view all serious spiritual work toward transformation as more scientific than religious in the commonly accepted sense. Unlike religion, science is always in ferment, always changing. No body of scientific knowledge is finally accepted by the most rigorous scientists to be more than provisional. In science there is always room for movement, growth, and change, and that's a good thing, because movement, growth, and change are always tending to take place.

I am reminded of one of Sir Isaac Newton's famous comments. Acknowledging the extraordinary range of his scientific vision, far exceeding that of those who preceded him, Newton said, "If I see far, it is because I am standing on the shoulders of giants."

That is how I feel about my own work, vis-a-vis all the great men and women of spiritual acumen and power who have ever lived, and especially with regard to my own immediate predecessor gurus in this lifetime. While I respect the integrity and the great accomplishments of these giants of the past and the present, I also find their contributions wanting. I do not suggest that they were or are lying or even deluded, but, yes, I do propose that they were, or are, misinterpreting the phenomena revealed by their own illumined observation.

Perhaps it is better to say that new understanding is now available which exposes limits in those previous interpretations. The science of human transformation has surpassed their current comprehension. It's not unlike the new perspective on Newtonian physics that, in the era of relativity and quantum mechanics, has become both possible and inevitable. Newton's view, once farthest reaching, is now included and appreciated within a more sophisticated intelligence that discerns yet farther horizons.

I see that a whole new degree of confidence in Being and communion with others and with All that IS has become possible for many people in our time. I am not trying to exalt myself. I often find it unnerving to have to take as strong a stand as I feel I must. In some ways I would prefer not to feel obliged to say these things. Even so, I must propose that I have spontaneously revealed a whole new way for human beings to integrate the transcendent and the immanent, the divine and the human, the infinite and the finite dimensions of our natures. I point clearly to my predecessors in this and all my other writings. But I also indicate what I feel are my own breakthroughs, achieved with the help of my stalwart and dedicated friends on the path, yet nonetheless first apprehended by me. And I feel that our breakthroughs break so decisively with all the forms of spiritual and conscious fulfillment that have been promulgated elsewhere and in other epochs that I can only speak of what we are realizing as a summary, concusive second birth and a radically new life for all who would and do partake.

As an example of this innovative understanding and the breakthroughs it initiates, take the point I made above, that confusion and separateness are natural, inevitable, and appropriate in the evolutionary cycle of human existence that I call the first birth. It takes standing in the vantage of the second birth in a particularly open-hearted way to see this. It also takes standing here to notice that nearly every human being on the planet is still very much at odds with this proposition. Every single ideology, belief system, and teaching that has appeared in human history contends, in one fashion or another, against our confusion and separateness. The most blatant and burdensome result of this is that we have inherited a planet swarming with ideas that function like an energetic and spiritual plague among members of our species. These ideas hold, at root, that our confusion and separateness prove there is something fundamentally wrong with each one of us.

Either these ideas propose that we are each living in "original sin" of one kind or another, or they suggest that, as long as confusion and separateness characterize our existence, we have not done the proper work to get liberated from them. Either we are inherently sinful, base, evil, deluded, and wrong, or, at the very least, we are not doing or have not completed the work it takes to achieve sinlessness, sublimity, goodness, enlightenment, and righteousness. More likely, if not inherently sinful and all but damned, we are held to be base, lazy, weak, and unavailable to our own salvation and liberation.

I am not proposing that confusion and separateness are wonderful and delightful, and that we should therefore just accept them and live with and as them. No, I am suggesting, instead, that it is altogether to our most profound advantage to enter into an understanding of our nature whereby we recognize and honor the naturalness, indeed the inevitability, and thus the inherent dignity, of these chronic qualities of our lives. Such understanding permits a deep acceptance of these qualities. That very acceptance, paradoxically, then permits a truly transformative process of recognition to occur over time – such that eventually those qualities fundamentally disappear from our existence.

Perhaps I am not making it clear to you yet how much of a

quantum shift in our perspective and behavior this orientation represents. It's aggravating to me that I only have the same old language, even if with a few new words and phrases, to try to communicate a vast new sensibility. The point I have broached in these last three paragraphs is one that I will craft and hone again and again, from all kinds of directions, in these pages and throughout all my teachings. Why? Because, as obvious as this notion may seem to the mind, its depth as a living reality will probably continue to elude you for a long time. Correct me if I turn out to be wrong, but my bet is that this one is huge for you. If you come and work with my friends and me in your realization and expression of Being, I expect it will be years before you finally can honor the inherent dignity and, yes, even utter divinity of the whole apparatus of your separateness and confusion. Long after you have entered your second birth, you will be recognizing and releasing the residual self-negating psychology that you had no choice but to construct on the helpless foundation of the core wound.

Whether or not the unimpeachable truth of this point I am making has begun to strike you, it certainly has struck me, and long ago. I have been contemplating the significance of this quantum shift for quite some time. As a result, I am confident that what I am presenting – not merely in words, but in effortless transmission of Being – presages and inaugurates an immense evolutionary transition for humanity. Thus, I am moved to predict that the age of first birth humanity is now ending. It cannot survive. It is becoming obsolete as I write, and as you read. Humanity is not – here is the old view again – sinfully avoiding its ultimate and true nature, its salvation, its liberation. Humanity has, for many good or at least inescapable reasons, been deprived till now of the opportunity to recognize our confusion and separateness, and to stand free and strong in our true and total Being.

At this evolutionary juncture, that opportunity is still so very new that hardly any human body even knows it is here. But its gospel travels body by body, announcing itself in freedom, creativity, fundamental wellness and integrity of wholly divine and wholly human being. Once it begins to sing, that voice of Being can never be silenced again, and its songs cannot help but reach around the globe and even through the universe, wherever we go, whomever we encounter, throughout our future.

As I write, perhaps only a couple of dozen, maybe a few dozen, human beings are consciously living in this second birth, this divinely human integrity and wellness of Being. The day will come when, as you read, there will be millions, even billions, doing so. Perhaps that day is generations, centuries, even millenia away. Nonetheless, I am confident that humanity will leap to grasp the opportunity as soon as it presents itself in an intelligent, credible, and trustworthy manner. Since that is now happening, even if only among a few prototype "models" of second birth awakeness, I venture this prediction and take my stand.

Humanity is not living in sin. Humanity is simply confused. Humanity is not resisting the necessary work that would bring salvation, liberation, divinity. Humanity is waiting to be welcomed into its inherently saved, free, and divine estate. Humanity does not need to struggle to lift itself out of its degradation and torpor. Humanity needs to be helped to fall into the Ground of Being and thence to stand forward in its unavoidable Truth, embodying the transcendent to the utmost degree, conscious as the immanent heart of matter, body by body, life by life, heart by heart.

Humanity needs to outgrow its first birth. The White-Hot Way of Mutuality, of Waking Down, is a school of such growth that is proving to be quite effective. First let me tell you why. Then I will tell you how. Not all of how, because it can't be told, but enough to whet your appetite, I hope.

On one level, you will need to come to me or another adept of the second birth awakeness, so that we can live the "how" to you in radiant silence (whether we are speaking or not).

On another, deeper level, however, the reason I cannot tell you the "how" is that you must discover most of it for yourself. In cooperation with me or someone like me, yes – but for, and by, yourself.

Seven

Beyond Hypermasculine Dharmas, or Lifeways, of Superimposed and Formulaic Seeking

To get into this particular consideration, I need to offer a judgment that some people will find difficult or impossible to agree with. Nonetheless, I have no choice but to say it just this way:

With respect to its promises and claims, till now, human religion and spirituality has been a disastrous, if not complete, failure.

I'm not proposing, you see, that spirituality has simply and only failed. It's obvious to me that our spiritual quests and faiths have made great, indeed seminal, contributions to human culture. But with regard to what it has claimed and promised to human beings, our spiritual legacy has failed us, and miserably.

Take a look around. The Jungian therapist James Hillman wrote a book recently titled, *One Hundred Years of Psychotherapy and the World Is Getting Worse.* We could well counter with, *Several Millenia of Religion and Spirituality and the World Is Not Really Getting Better.* "Worse"? "Better"? "No change"? Well, I don't really know how to determine criteria for agreeing about these matters anyway.

All I can say is, I listen to the daily news a lot more carefully than I do the latest predictions from the Pleiades. All around me people are confident that everything is just getting peachy – that a massive infusion of divine Light and Wisdom is happening all over the planet and making it so that everyone everywhere will soon gracefully evolve into bodies of radiant joy. Or that this guru or that teacher's work has made changes in the world-process such that great numbers will simply awaken spontaneously to their essential, free consciousness and then live in freedom thereafter. I've never been able to swallow these notions. They sound to me like the millenialism that afflicted western Europe now just exactly a thousand years ago.

When I say that I feel that the evolutionary heyday of the first birth is now ending, and that great numbers of people will soon awaken, I am not depending upon any stellar infusion of divine grace. I am depending upon *us*, body by body, person by person, heart by heart. I am not talking about vicarious mass salvation. I am talking about inheritance of both the opportunity and the obligation to take total, divinely human responsibility, each human one by each human one.

I do feel that humanity is rapidly outgrowing its previous evolutionary templates. But the manner of the real, authentic outgrowing will require an individual and cooperative assumption of responsibility and clear-eyed wisdom for which no mass empowerment can compensate. I do believe that there is a "critical mass" factor to this evolutionary leap. But I don't feel that it will manifest fully like a flash flood roaring through a town. It will work, I think, more like a benign contagion. People will catch on more and more quickly, yes. But then they will discover that a grand enterprise of unavoidable and often extremely difficult work stands before them. And they will first discover and then accomplish that work one by one, with no guarantees of success and many obstacles and pitfalls ahead.

What is the nature of the contagion? One way to characterize it is via the terms I use in the title of this chapter. It is a passage beyond helpless domination by, and fealty to, what I call the hypermasculine dharmas of dissociation and superimposed, formulaic seeking.

First, let me offer some further definitions here. (As you may recall, I also treated this topic in the Prologue.) I came up with the term hypermasculine out of simultaneous sympathy and exasperation with the frequently pejorative use, these days, of the term patriarchal. Patriarchs and patriarchal orientations are as natural and ordinary to human affairs as their female, matriarchal counterparts. These terms should dignify the responsible wisdom and power of human elders. They shouldn't, I feel, be burdened with negative connotations.

Hypermasculine, by contrast, serves well without automatically demonizing anyone who happens, in his family or domain, to be a patriarch or a patriarchal man. We may define it as follows: the hypermasculine orientation in human individuals and groups involves the tendencies toward dissociation from the body, the physical world, ordinary human reactions, desires, feelings, activities, and relationships, for the sake of either control of or liberation from embodied life and material conditions, or even all phenomenal Nature.

The masculine impulse in our natures seeks to analyze, control, govern, grasp, and penetrate. In order to do any or all of these, it must first differentiate itself from that to which it seeks to do such things. When the masculine impulse achieves excessive dominance in an individual, a group, a civilization, then its necessary urge toward differentiation and autonomy becomes hypermasculine: dissociative, self-isolating, and alienated from that from which it is differentiating. That dissociative urge, taken to the extreme, becomes obsessed with an absolute severance of relatedness to all that is felt to be "other," different, threatening, binding.

The urges to analyze, control, govern, grasp, and penetrate, if not put to the service of the extreme desire for a dissociation that severs all ties, can still achieve their own hypermasculine extremes. They then become obsessive forces that tend to stifle, suppress, violate, and tyrannize that from which the hypermasculine mind or psyche has become detached.

What does the hypermasculine impulse distance itself from, and then relate to with such aggression or violence? The body. The natural world. The sluggish, restrictive limits of material and phenomenal Nature. Matter. "Mater" – the female, the feminine in all its forms. That which is dark, deep, hidden, unconscious. That which is instinctual, uncivilized, out of rational control.

The hypermasculine quality is much more deeply ingrained and influential in our lives than might initially appear obvious. In *The White-Hot Yoga of the Heart,* I spoke of it as the necessary and inevitable culture-making force that has dominated humanity for at least the last five to ten thousand years, resulting in two primary cultural archetypes or manifestations:

> What [has been described] as the "primordial unconscious unity" [of human prehistory] is the early human cultural format that, by contrast, we could call "hyperfeminine." Humanity has had to pull itself up into hypermasculine cultural arcs in order to convert its cultural force from forms primarily expressive of the elements of earth and water (static or conservative geological and biological forces) to those expressive of the elements of fire and air (dynamic,

> transformative, and transcendental geological and
> biological forces). . . .
>
> The hypermasculine arc of classically Western
> culture has sought to liberate the human psyche and
> body *within* or in active relation to material – "Mater-
> ial," dominantly feminine – Nature.

Perhaps the most obvious classically Western cultural arc of
hypermasculinity has been the revolutions in scientific knowledge
and technology that have changed the whole world in the last several centuries. The hypermasculine psyche in its Western mode is
not trying to get away from material and phenomenal Nature. No,
it is only trying to understand it and thence, by rational and forceful means, to control, alter, and in general to govern and exploit it.

> The hypermasculine arc of classically Eastern
> culture has sought to liberate the human conscious-
> ness *from* or in active dissociation from material
> Nature, including, even particularly, the material
> human body and materially based human psyche.

In contrast to its Western counterpart, the most obvious
classically Eastern cultural arc of hypermasculinity has been the long-
standing Oriental impulse toward liberation from this world and all
the pain and suffering associated with it.

Both of these hypermasculine arcs of culture are alive in each
and every one of our bodies and psyches. Each, I suggest, is
profoundly dissociative, the one in order to control, the other in
order to separate from and be free of, those fleshy, material,
stubbornly assertive features of our lives that human beings find so
fascinating and troublesome: sex, desire, money, emotions, actual
personal relationships, and the like.

The reason I am taking time to define this term more fully here
is because, from the perspective of this White-Hot Way of Mutuality, literally *all* previously elaborated secular, religious, spiritual, and
transcendent paths wind up revealing their hypermasculine imbalances and governing dispositions. When you begin to Wake Down,
first into helpless existence *as* the core wound of confusion and separateness, you are actually falling out of the whole hypermasculine
way of being alive. You are not merely losing control of your life.
You are losing the illusion of such control. This is not failure, or
regression. It is an evolutionary advance, it is progress, but it doesn't

often feel that way.

The word "dharma," as I understand it, helps us appreciate this evolutionary passage. Dharma is a Sanskrit word. I am not interested in trying to get everyone to increase the Sanskrit in their vocabulary, and I will go to great lengths to avoid any non-English language terms in my teaching. Yet I have found no way to avoid using this word.

Since ancient times, Dharma with a capital "D" has been understood in Sanskrit-based languages as "the teaching of Truth," "the ultimate Law of existence," or "the supreme Way of liberation." And, when written with a lower case "d," the same word has been understood to mean "one's duty, path, calling, or appropriate and natural ways of participating in life." Capitalized, the word thus refers, traditionally, to the Law or "the Way it is and must be" for all human beings, indeed all beings. Uncapitalized, the same term refers to the law, way, path, or true place, lot, and lifeway of any particular individual.

In recent years, however, it has come to my attention that the root meaning of the word dharma is "that which sustains." This definition seems much more cogent to me than any of the others. It appears to me to be the meaning that underlies all the others, whether the word is used in its capitalized form or not. It's in this sense that I find I must use this particular Sanskrit word in my own work. (There are a few other Sanskrit terms that will come up here and there, too, and for similar reasons.) There is simply no adequate equivalent in English. "Teaching" does not say it. "Law" does not say it. "Path" and "duty" do not say it. "Way" and even "lifeway" do not encompass the whole meaning of the word.

I suggest that if we trace the lines of human history, we see that hypermasculine dharmas arose as inevitable and entirely necessary reactions to the hyperfeminine condition of early humanity. In the hyperfeminine, prehistoric epochs, we were embedded in material Nature. We had not profoundly differentiated ourselves from the world-stuff that surrounded us and pervaded our bodies. It is not that hyperfeminine or prehistoric humanity had no intelligent comprehension of its own nature. No, it is just that that comprehension ultimately did not suffice.

Hyperfeminine humanity perceived, and still perceives where it has survived, that human beings fit into the cycle of material and psychic natural conditions in a particular way. We are subordinate to ancestors, to angelic and godlike beings, and to the mysterious

Creator of everything. We are in harmonious, rhythmic brotherhood and sisterhood with other living creatures. Like them, we feed on other creatures and eventually, in death, are returned to yet other creatures as food. Every living thing is a spirit, and every part of material Nature is alive. The world is thus made of Spirit, and the human being is meant to live in harmony with his or her world through an overall dharma, we could say, of cooperation, both humble and proud of our place in the natural cycles of life and death.

This kind of understanding persists today in the spiritual teachings and lore of indigenous peoples all over the world. Its great exemplars and adepts, historically, have been shamans. These natural mystics were not without a recognition of the subtler possibilities of human experience. On the contrary, they were schooled and skilled in such explorations. But their spirituality assumed that the human spirit's most appropriate concerns were to live in right balance and harmony with all of Nature, as well as with one's family, clan, and tribe. Their spirituality did not seek any kind of salvation or liberation from Nature, nor did any aspect of their lifeways attempt to exert any kind of control over Nature.

This is where the hypermasculine force arose in human beings and became, gradually, predominant. The indigenous life-ways were essentially passive, receptive, and subordinated to laws of Nature that kept human beings in a certain place in the circles of life and death. At some point, in many sectors of the world, human beings began to come alive with a new impulse. They began to feel, perceive, and articulate a need, and then a capacity, to extricate themselves spiritually, mentally, and emotionally from the hyperfeminine context of prehistoric existence.

They began to conceive of gods that were superior to the spirit-forces of the sun, the wind, and fire, and they began to yearn to realize god-like states of liberation from being embedded in this world of inevitable birth, suffering, sickness, old age, and death. At approximately the same time, and sometimes in the same cultures, they began to conceive of ways to manipulate, control, and use natural forces that made them capable of godlike transformations of the stuff of Nature itself.

As I wrote above, one of these hypermasculine arcs took what has become a classically Oriental form. It attempts to liberate human consciousness from what we might call the "embed" of bodily, emotional, mental, and relational cycles of birth, life, and death, by physical and mental, as well as spiritual and conscious,

45

technologies of escape.

The other arc took what we can now see, in our age, as a classically Occidental form. It attempts to liberate the human mind and body within that same embed of cyclic existence (even if the cycle is perceived to last for only one lifetime), by physical and mental technologies of control.

The classically Oriental way is always trying to get liberated from "the wheel of birth and death." Many Western teachings have similar goals, but historically, at least some of them have Oriental antecedents. The classically Occidental approach is always trying to get control over, or to conquer, all forms of material Nature. Many Eastern societies have demonstrated similar impulses, but, especially nowadays, much of that movement has come back to them from the West.

I propose that if we look closely at both of these arcs of hypermasculine culture, all over the world, we will find several salient characteristics almost everywhere we turn. Whether classically Oriental or classically Occidental, or, as is most often the case, some combination of the two, the hypermasculine cultural force has always been at root a *dissociative* intelligence and energy. As a dharma, in other words, as a sustaining force in human consciousness and life, the hypermasculine impulse fundamentally works to extricate us from the limits of our embeddedness in the-world-as-we-have-known-it-to-be.

This is not, I suggest, merely some negative development of which we must be healed. That is where I take issue with teachings today that merely preach a return to the harmonies of the indigenous peoples. Humanity has needed to extricate itself from those forms of embeddedness. There is more to the human being than such teachings and cultures would cede. They served well in the time of hyperfeminine awakening to our existence in and as part of the world. But they ceased to accommodate All of Who we are, each and together, long ago. Therefore, they had to be countered and then, eventually, dominated by the hypermasculine reaction that arose all across the Earth.

Where we have been unconsciously associated with the world-stuff, the hypermasculine cultural impulse has arisen with a first and ever fundamental intention to *dissociate* from perceived limits on who we are and what we can be and do. That intention has then produced other salient and nearly universal characteristics of the hypermasculine dharmas.

In order to accomplish the necessary dissociation, extrication, or liberation, the hypermasculine force of Being first analyzes the limits it perceives and then deduces, by both intuitive and deductive means, strategies of thought and action that will achieve the desired goals. The hypermasculine impulse then works to *superimpose* these strategic *formulas* of thought and action upon the living human body and mind. An effort is made to replace previously active patterns of thought and action that are perceived to reinforce the limits of the status quo.

Thus, to summarize, the emerging hypermasculine impulse first feels or perceives that previously natural and acceptable patterns of being, thinking, and acting now communicate somehow unacceptable limits upon human nature and possibility. It then struggles spontaneously to dissociate itself from the binding force of those limits. In that struggle, it must analyze the nature of the limits and then find and superimpose upon itself formulas for how to think and to act – and, indeed, how to be – that will allow its fullest possible liberation from or perhaps within the field of those limits.

Whether it produces a scientific formula, a mystic vision, a skyscraper, a hybrid peach, a love poem, a child, a yogic power, or a spontaneous realization of spiritual freedom, this is how the hypermasculine impulse operates.

As long as humanity has fundamentally needed to exercise the hypermasculine reaction to its perceived limitations of embeddedness in natural or previously existing cultural conditions, the hypermasculine impulse has made for true dharma all over the world. Since prehistoric times, all of our spiritual and intellectual philosophies, all of our methods of teaching and learning, all of our patterns for achieving dominance in and with respect to the material world or liberation from its cycles, have been cast in the hypermasculine mold. Every great religion and every great scientific technology has these characteristics. Even religious appeals to divine grace and spiritual acts of discipleship and meditation are classically formulaic and superimposed.

It might be argued that the hyperfeminine world had its own superimposed and formulaic strategies of seeking to achieve certain qualities of existence or effects of change in material Nature. True enough. But before the appearance of the hypermasculine impulse, I suggest, in whatever cultural format such strategies operated, they too were universally perceived by the participants as *the way it always was.* Listen to the teachings, even today, of indigenous shamans and native peoples. There is a brokenhearted nostalgia for how things used to be for human beings when things were still the way they always had been.

Nowadays, even such nostalgic yearnings have their own hypermasculine quality. What is being yearned for is no longer the natural, actual reality of the world. Thus, these yearnings grope for what is not presently possible. They exist in dissociative reaction to the hypermasculine world conditions and dharmas that surround them. Those who turn to such cultural schools are desperately trying to superimpose the past upon the present. The world has become a hypermasculine province over these last many thousands of years, and the hyperfeminine ways of old cannot survive intact.

What I have provided in this chapter is a fairly abstract analysis. Over the course of this book you will see much more vividly, I hope, how the hypermasculine motions of strategic dissociation and superimposed, formulaic thought and action have formed the basis of nearly every kind of seeking that is now available. And I hope to help you feel how humanity is now beginning to stir from the curious, anxious dreams that such seeking has made our chronic experience.

In our epoch, the hypermasculine impulse itself has become, to my view, the limiting embed from which Being now is struggling to extricate itself in human form. But that struggle does not and indeed cannot proceed through yet other forms of hypermasculine analysis and superimposition of formulas of practice: meditate thus, act thus, think thus, feel thus; do this and do not do that.

Rather, the present struggle of Being to extricate itself from hypermasculine limits and imbalances proceeds through one means alone, which no body could or would possibly choose to superimpose upon itself, and which is utterly non-formulaic.

I call that means "the Rot." It is the way whereby human beings fall out of hypermasculine fixation in states of the mind or the soul-nature and their patterns of seeking, and into helpless acceptance of the core wound of confusion and separateness as a supreme, albeit transitional, realization of Who we are.

This passage is the beginning of real surrender into conscious embodiment. And it is the natural way in Being whereby we human beings emerge from both hyperfeminine and hypermasculine imbalances into the true harmony of divinely human integration, in both our identity and our relatedness.

Eight

The Rot: Out of Head-Mind-Soul Awareness and into Heart-Body-Consciousness

The Rot is the passage that individuals undergo when they conclusively begin to lose faith in – and enthusiasm for – the hopes, beliefs, enterprises, and all the personal, social, and cultural forms whereby they have engaged in an endless search for happiness, peace, freedom, love, enlightenment, or other ultimate or even ordinary goals in life.

The passage beyond hypermasculine dissociation and idealistic seeking really begins with the Rotting away of everything you have ever been able to do to better yourself, to succeed, to get what you want, to get free. More precisely, it begins with your fundamental loss of ultimate hope in all such things. You may continue with your meditation, your therapy; you most likely will maintain your responsibilities to family and friends; you most likely won't abandon your job, your career, and other activities. But at the center of the whole great symphony of your own life, you begin to notice and helplessly endure a stunned, stark silence, an emptiness, a despair.

All of your life you have been seeking, often quite aggressively, to overcome this silent desolation at the core. When the Rot really sets in, nothing works any more. It may feel to you as if you are losing everything you have ever gained. It may appear that you are becoming the opposite of a spiritual person, a responsible citizen, family member, whatever. In fact, most people are able to keep their lives more or less together. But right at the very core of everything, a disintegration of hope and confidence sets in and will not lift.

Different people Rot in different ways. (I have to capitalize references to this process – it is so thoroughly sacred and divine. Yet we usually experience it as anything but that!) Some people go through dramatic and difficult ordeals that chasten them into readiness to permit the Rot to do its work. Others appear to be breezing through life as if no problem had ever occurred, as if nothing were wrong, out of place, incomplete or frustrating. Yet, regardless of the surface appearances, the Rot goes on in all those who can no longer avoid it. Because, as many of my friends have agreed, as long as you can avoid the Rot, you will.

I have seen this to be so, again and again. As long as you have a path, as long as you have anxious hope, as long as you have a trajectory that you're traveling, an arc of growth to cultivate and defend, you are not yet prepared to encounter and embrace existence as the core wound. Therefore, you will not permit yourself to endure the onset and the consequences of the Rot.

A couple of years ago, I spent some time serving a man who is a meditation teacher. He was attracted to what I was saying, but only, I sensed, in a kind of romantic way. Sure enough, as soon as the natural phenomena of this process began to appear in him, he bolted. He described how everything was fine, except that when he woke up each morning, he felt himself falling into a dark swamp of despair that he could not get out of, no matter how hard he tried. I attempted to help him accept the swamp and its despair, to give up and sink into it and just be there, even if he might feel as if he were drowning. But he was not ready for that passage. And shortly thereafter our work together ended, at least for an indefinite time.

What makes the Rot an evolutionary crisis is not the mere fact that things no longer appear to be working for you. Rather, it is where you are Rotting from, and what you are Rotting into. In *The White-Hot Yoga of the Heart* I speak of these matters in terms of centers of identity-gravity. As long as you are still fundamentally activated in the hypermasculine mode, the center of identity to which you gravitate, and from which you chronically view the world, is more or less analogous to the head. Its seat is the mind or total psyche, and its active essence or core is the individuated soul-nature, the root feeling of "I" or "me" that persists through all the ordinary states of daily waking, dreaming, and sleeping. This is true even of individuals who appear to be based in the heart, the emotional being or body, or in the physical, material, elemental body. I am talking about a deeper dimension of chronic identity than where any person's characteristic concentration of life-force happens to manifest.

The person who is authentically involved in the Rot is falling, steadily and most often helplessly, out of the idealistic, dissociative, anxious mode of superimposed and formulaic seeking, and into the realistic, naturally associative, and more and more peaceful mode of participation in what IS in his or her life. A shift is occurring, in other words, in his or her characteristic place and orientation of identity.

What is happening? He or she is "dropping," as my friends like to say, out of head-mind-soul awareness and into Heart-body-consciousness. He or she is falling into existence *as* the core wound of confusion and separateness. This drop cannot be willed, motivated, made to happen by any means whatsoever. It occurs only via the Rot.

The most dangerous way to relate to it is to imagine that you have already done it just because you have done a lot of inner work of a deep, psychological and spiritual kind. Then you can fool yourself, and thus deprive yourself of a realistic reckoning with your nature.

This is a big point, or, better to say, a huge red flag. I have had so many experiences of people coming to me and, when I start talking about the Rot, nodding their heads with a smile that is at once rueful, humbled – and incredibly proud. "Yep – I sure know what that is. Been there. Done that. Don't need any more Rot, no sirree."

In general, after that, one of two things has occurred. Either they are never really touched by my transmission, so that the Being-force never activates in them in such a way that they drop into the stark actuality of their persisting, underlying distress. Or, if they finally do somehow permit themselves to be touched in that way, they find something wrong with me and the work itself, or the community of participants, and thus rationalize a righteous departure.

I am not begrudging such individuals their need to make their own ways through life, which include holding whatever opinions of my work and of me that they will or must. I am simply saying that I have seen a small parade of great souls come through my door and go out again without ever having understood what I actually mean when I speak of the core wound, the hypermasculine patterns of dissociation and seeking, and, especially, the Rot.

When the true Rot is under way, whether the conditions of the person's life appear positive or negative, whether he or she appears happy, calm, sane, and functional, or exactly the opposite, a kind of composting is occurring in the very heart or core of the being. The person's previous beliefs, pursuits, paths, and achievements have already provided all the nurturance they can. Now they exist as a form of refuse, organic garbage of the soul, we might say. Indeed, in a sense the soul-nature itself is the compost heap, and the essence of the composting matter too! All of this material is fertilizer that is then naturally distributed to lend nutrients to the newly germinating, living seed of true and total Being.

How it all works is mysterious. Something that used to be essential now Rots away. And some new essential thing comes to life by feeding upon that former essence, or one's no longer viable relationship to it.

We need to clarify something here. It's not as if, after Rotting in this manner, you never try to do anything to better your life ever again. Hardly. You may become impassioned to change many aspects of both your own life and others' lives. But you will have ceased to do so as an effort to relieve yourself of that underlying emptiness or despair. You will have ceased to seek in fundamental reaction to the core wound.

You will have experienced, instead, a transmission of divinely human identity and relatedness from one or more competent adepts – and that transmission will have shown you how to begin living in freedom from such fundamental reactivity.

Nine

Transmission and the Adept's Job

W hat is "transmission"? And, what is an "adept"? I've used these terms already, and spoken of these matters briefly before. Now let's get into them more completely. I want to approach answers to these questions in response to the needs of someone who is in the Rot, rather than approach them in the abstract.

As I indicated in the previous chapter, the Rot is no picnic, whether you are capable of smiles and laughter or not. People read about mystic passages such as "the dark night of the soul" and romanticize them, but, whatever the mystics may mean when they speak of such trials, the actual experience of the Rot never comes with a merit badge and a pat on the back from Being. It communicates itself as exhaustion, despair, an onset of hopelessness, an incapacity to muster up the energy for even one more meditative technique, one more promising therapy, one more exciting new avenue of growth and change. When you are falling into or drowning in the Rot, your world becomes rather gray and pale, even while others around you appear cheery, bright, and full of life. You may become convinced that you can't accomplish any change in yourself at all. You may feel like a complete failure at whatever it is you've been so intent upon, whether a spiritual path, family life, your career, love, relationships, an artistic, athletic, or scientific endeavor, or anything else.

I can't count the number of people who have walked through the door into my sessions of meditation and conversation and cautioned me out front that they were really not interested in finding another teacher. So many times the deep despair of the Rot has spoken to me face to face, saying, in effect, "Forget it. I can't be helped. I don't have what it takes. Everything has failed for me. I am here because I felt I had to come check you out, but I really don't want a guru, a path. I don't even know if I want enlightenment or freedom. I don't even know if those things exist. I just don't know."

Such people have often spent time cultivating the attitude of no-seeking. Many traditional teachings and any number of pop, New Age enthusiasms encourage people to just accept things as they are, don't search, "go with the flow," and so on. But cultivating such attitudes is, to my view, another form of hypermasculine seeking. It's actually an extremely dangerous one. It often breeds deep cynicism and resentment, because the enterprise, for most people, is inherently self-sabotaging. To "try not to seek" is like "trying not to think of a tree." The very attempt is its own failure. And even while the mind of the seeker, or the would-be non-seeker, tries to keep believing it will achieve the goal some day, the heart and whole being suffer the conflicting motivations and built-in frustration of the entire adventure.

I suggest to you that the true end of seeking – that is, of anxious questing to solve or overcome the core wound of confusion and separateness – is none other than the Rot. But when that end of seeking is taking form in the heart of your being, it feels like anything but a successful spiritual quest to end seeking. You may see friends around you who say they have really completed their journey, seeking is over, they are free. Then you look at yourself and you see a confused mess. You see a failed quest. You see a casualty of the quest, someone gazing wistfully toward what must be heaven from outside a barbed-wire fence. Such a person is not likely to be capable of enthusiasm for the next great expedition toward the goal.

This is where the transmission, as well as the good counsel and instruction, of a true adept becomes crucial.

What I mean by transmission is that person's effortless and spontaneous radiation of the bodily realization of Being. I am not talking merely about a tangible energy or presence that you may feel around such a person, or when you think of them – though such energy or presence may likely be palpable to you. Nor am I talking about anything that any such person can or would intentionally broadcast, as if by somehow turning on a switch in themselves. Yet this radiation of awakened and awakening Being-force is a transmission. It is a tangible energy or presence, to be sure, but its most distinctive characteristic is that of embodied conscious identity and feeling. This transmission comes from one body, that of the awakened adept, and it goes to another, that of the aspirant. And if the aspirant is truly Rotting, then that transmission of Being-force can be most fully and easily received. The aspirant may not even know very much about this reception at first. Nonetheless, it happens, and once it happens it begins to transform that person's life from the heart out.

Thus, transmission is a kind of paradox. I can say that it does appear that something comes from one body and enters another. But it might be more accurate to say that the one body, that of the aspirant, templates upon that of the other, the adept. The aspiring one is "breathing toward" the adept one, the one who evinces natural mastery. The aspirant finds the adept attractive in a most potent way. His or her own latent or just emerging realization of true and total Being becomes magnetized, or templated upon, the adept's mature, profoundly expressed, and radiant quality of that very realization.

An analogy occurs to me that might be helpful. (Usually, all such analogies eventually reveal their limits and weaknesses, but we'll see where this one goes.) Probably, with all the many movies that make drama of such things, you have watched scenes where a jet fighter is lining up another plane as a target. On the console is a screen, and when the target is lined up properly, the screen indicates that the target is now in "missile lock." Then, no matter what feinting maneuvers the other plane might attempt, once the missile is fired it cannot help but find its target.

Well, in the templating process of transmission, the crucial event that must occur is that adept and aspirant must each locate each other in a benign, human form of missile lock. Once that is done, it is not exactly as if anything gets "fired," though there do need to be occasions wherein they sit contemplating Being together without the distractions of speech and activity. The sheer fact of being in one another's sights this way makes the transmission not only possible but actual. Moreover, it is not only activated when they are physically in the same space. Once activated, it goes on continuously, twenty-four hours a day, regardless of what either of them is doing in, as, and with body and mind.

There is, however, a differential with regard to capacity. The adept does not need to do anything to be accomplishing the transmission. In a sense, then, he or she is always making an unbroken communication of freedom and peace in the Onlyness of Being. The aspirant, on the other hand, is not always conscious of that communication, and needs to cultivate his or her availability to it. Especially in the early stages, the aspirant's screen on the console registers interruptions. It appears to go out of missile lock. And then he or she must work to recapture the "target."

This analogy is probably wearing thin for you; it certainly is for me. What are we looking at here?

The person who is Rotting out of the hypermasculine stage of human evolution cannot activate will or effort in the old ways any more. He or she may try, indeed may experience an endless reflexive revisitation of the old ways of seeking, grasping, struggling, and trying. No such efforts will avail. Therefore, what is necessary is to come into contact with someone who is already living in the condition that is free of such hypermasculine efforting, who radiates that freedom as naturally as the sun radiates light. That contact has to be worked by both parties. The aspirant needs to feed on the adept's freedom until he or she has metabolized it and made it his or her own. The adept needs to make sure to give the aspirant every necessary and fruitful opportunity he or she can find to do so.

What I mean by "adept," you see, is something very specific to the White-Hot Way of Mutuality. There are all kinds of adepts in the world. Anyone who is competent at any task might be said to be an adept of it. And there are all kinds of spiritual teachers, gurus, lamas, rabbis, priests, shamans, mystics, yogis, sages, prophets, healers, channelers, avatars, and saints who are adepts of one or another state of religious or spiritual illumination, salvation, or freedom.

The nature of an adept in the White-Hot Way of Mutuality, of which I am the founding and originating adept, is someone who has healed his or her core wound of fundamental confusion in identity and fundamental separateness in relations. He or she has done so to such a degree that there is no essential doubt about it. Moreover, he or she lives in such a fashion that others naturally feel this freedom, this fundamental wellness of Being, and gravitate to it. The wellness, you see, is contagious, and those who are realized adepts of it spontaneously infect others with it. The adepts' job is to find ways natural to them to exercise that process of transmission, give it form, and ensure its effectiveness for others.

In other words, such an adept must continually find ways to maximize the utility of his or her natural, unwilled transmission of awakened wellness of Being. A lot of that work, in this White-Hot Way of Mutuality, consists of helping the aspirant recognize and stand free of binding illusions, misconceptions, and prejudices about what existence is, and how realization or awakened life is supposed to be.

Another major portion of the work is to help the aspirant feel down into the dark, confused, and disturbed patterns of his or her subconscious and unconscious conditioning. To do this, the adept must be willing to meet the aspirant in the midst of whatever he or she is feeling.

This is in sharp contrast to the hypermasculine modes of teaching, which always tend to make us wrong. They cut us off from simple acceptance of ourselves in the most constricted and agonized aspects of our nature. They are always telling us to meditate more, work on ourselves more, change, outgrow.

The adept who embraces mutuality must meet you in all the places of your self that you have previously avoided, disallowed, and tried to keep hidden, even from your self. But he or she does more than this. The adept must allow you to see and experience him or her in those same reactive spaces, or similar ones. This is one of the most empowering parts of the work of the adept – enabling the aspirant to encounter and respond to his or her own reactive, shadow life.

I have said many times that this work is not about perfecting the body-mind. This is as true for adepts as it is for aspirants. Later in the book I'll talk more about how the awakened whole being of the adept-realizer does naturally refine itself over time, so that old patterns cease to appear much, if at all. But it's important for everyone contemplating this Way to grasp that awakening does not perfect the person of the adept.

In fact, understanding this may accelerate your own awakening. When you begin to get that the adept or adepts you are working with are not perfect and don't need to be, then you can also begin to relax your struggles to make yourself other than however you are already tending to be. And you allow yourself to begin to comprehend your nature from a disposition of deeper acceptance than you ever imagined possible.

Let me close this chapter from another perspective. Another word for adept, of course, is "guru." Anything that is even remotely associated with "guru" comes under suspicion these days as being a "cult." And all such things are negatively charged these days in general society – so much so that people tend to shy away even from what might be of great help to them. As you read more about the White-Hot Way of Mutuality, I hope you will see how my friends and I are attempting to bring a very beautiful baby out of the often very dirty bathwater of the traditions of gurus and disciples and the intentional gatherings of such beings that many people tend to label – and fear – as cults.

This clarifying enterprise is of utmost importance for human-ity. If the whole old way of being, the hypermasculine apparatus of personhood and cultural life, is to dissolve so that the core wound of separateness and confusion can be healed – and I propose that indeed it must – then somehow one must be able to receive a transfusion of the new life and disposition that allows such healing. Except in the rarest of cases, this cannot occur without transmis-sion. I have not seen it yet, nor have I heard any reliable instance of any such thing. Though I am the originator of the unique transmis-sion of realization beyond the hypermasculine, I also received my own primary adept's transmission for years.

Thus, the ancient dynamic of adept and aspirant must be refreshed and activated to serve the flowering of new life beyond the hypermasculine mode. But this historic adept/aspirant dynamic has for millenia existed in the context of, and in service to, that very hypermasculine mode of being. How can such transmission be effective without the stimulation of the same old dissociative limits and formulaic liabilities?

In a word: mutuality.

Ten

Mutuality and the Coconut Yoga

M utuality, in this particular school of White-Hot or
most intensely conscious embodiment, involves being true to your own true and total Self in all
communication and action, while simultaneously honoring and
cooperating with others who are doing the same themselves.

Most pictures of realized existence that we receive through the
hypermasculine traditions show us a view of the awakened individual and his or her traits or qualities of character. Two aspects of
these views seem gravely unreal and distorted to me. The first is
that the individual is seen as if isolated unto himself (hardly ever
unto "herself," but that is a whole other road we won't walk just
now). The realized one exists like a star, shining alone with his
enlightened qualities in an abstraction of non-relatedness. If there
are planets around, they're at a distance. Other stars? Light-years
away.

The second distortion has to do with those enlightened qualities.
The realized one is assumed to be more than just compas-
sionate, detached, wise, non-reactive, and so on. No, he or she is
supposed to be completely free of desire, anger, fear, doubt,
jealousy, and greed; smilingly stoic in the face of all adversity, even
unto death; unfailingly without a retaliatory bone in his or her body.

I make no bones about the inadequacy and irrelevance of those
pictures to the kind of awakened existence that appears among my
friends and me in this Way. Ours is a different kind of freedom. Its
hallmarks are not limited to inherent traits that can be assigned to
the individual. Rather, its hallmarks, especially in the domain of
relatedness, have to do with each one's active and sustained
practice of mutuality. And those characteristic traits have nothing to
do with superhuman detachment from real human feelings,
reactions, impulses, and desires.

Not long ago a woman I know was talking with me about her
process of awakening. We had been meeting on a one-to-one basis

for some weeks because she had found it unworkable to attend and participate with others in a group setting. I was willing to adapt our work together to her needs, although I knew at some point she would likely have to turn again to face and work through her difficulties with some particular others.

For some weeks, I counseled her with regard to the subjective or interior quality of her conscious existence. Our conversations had been fruitful, to a degree. Now, it had become evident to her that she was not moving in her process as she wished. She felt stuck, and she appealed to me to see if I could shed any light on her predicament.

At that point I felt no more room in me to help her refine her understanding of consciousness and its relationship in general to all phenomena. It appeared fruitless to put any more attention on identity, when she was so obviously out of sync in quite a number of important – if not especially close – relationships. And I encouraged her to really practice mutuality in those contexts.

She replied that she was doing so. She gave an example. She and a man, who is also active in my work, had been having a disagreement. Finally it flared up in such a volatile way that they could no longer even try to talk about it. The issue was just too sensitive to address. They agreed to just let it stand as they went on with the rest of what they chose to interact about.

I said, "Great story – but what you and he agreed and then chose to do has nothing to do with what I mean by mutuality." She was amazed. "What do you mean?"

I explained. "Mutuality includes all kinds of agreements, yes, and all kinds of interactions. But the essence of it is what you and another party do in the tight squeezes of relating, when it appears that there is no way to make any headway between you, and when the absolutely last thing you want to attempt is to actually get through to each other.

"That kind of moment is when the rubber of mutuality really hits the road. It is to dare to keep communicating – not to back away, not to 'agree to disagree,' but to keep daring to find a way to touch one another's hearts, and to let your own heart be touched, right in and through the deep places of pain and dissonance."

This kind of discussion may seem rudimentary to anyone who has done substantial psychological and emotional work to awaken and grow. All I can say is, when the great ordeal of Waking Down gets underway, these things take on new and startling significance. You discover that what you used to be doing was a form of working on yourself and your relationships from a distance. Now, however, you are more and more simply *here*, and the stakes and potential consequences of every communication magnify beyond what you could previously imagine possible.

In order to expedite and ease my friends' (and my own!) exercise of this stark commitment to relating with others, I have proposed that we each and all practice what I call "the Coconut Yoga." What it requires is the capacity, especially when two or more of your friends start flashing red flags of warning in your direction, to allow your forehead (and all your opinions, objections, defenses, and prejudices) to hit the ground like a coconut falling and cracking against a rock. In a word: surrender. In two words: bow down.

Two or more of any of your friends is a good rule of thumb, but I am pointing most to those who share your way of sacred living. Others may not be able to recognize and meet All of you sufficiently for you to be able to entrust yourself to them in this mode of surrender and receptivity. But among those who practice the White-Hot Way of Mutuality with you . . . well, again as a rule of thumb, any and every body counts. "Every body" includes not only the adepts you work with, but also your peers, those who are newer to the work, and your elders in the Way.

I want to emphasize that this practice of the Coconut Yoga is not just for people who are trying to awaken. It is for everyone: aspirants, realizers, and adepts. This practice appropriately levels us all. It reduces each one to the truly common places of Being with everyone else. Done right, it never fails to honor every body's dignity and every body's divinity. The Coconut Yoga balances identity and relatedness in situations that otherwise tend to bring out and polarize imbalances.

Without going into a lot of detail here, I must say that there is a vast difference between an adept who is practicing this yoga of vulnerability and one who is relating to others in the traditional, hypermasculine, divinely invulnerable position.

This doesn't mean that traditional adepts are merely immune and detached. Individuals who enjoy significant realization and perform adept service are likely to experience severe vulnerability as a continuous, personal, subjective condition. In other words, they find themselves often excruciatingly sensitive to their interactions with others, both physically and psychically. The traditional, hypermasculine modes of working encourage such individuals to immunize themselves from unnecessary exposure to and abuse by their disciples' unconsciousness. The methods of immunity typically consist of protocols of sacred etiquette that exalt the realizers and subordinate the aspirants. Living within the protective barriers of these protocols, the adepts are guaranteed at least sincere attempts at appropriate honoring of their spiritual and transcendent natures by those who have not achieved comparable awakenings. And they are also guaranteed freedom from intrusion by the emotional and psychological reactions and prejudices of those un-awakened beings.

I sympathize with the feelings and reactions that have tended to evoke such sociocultural norms in spiritual societies. But I also see that they can no longer be allowed to determine or govern sacred interaction and culture, as they have historically.

In the White-Hot Way of Mutuality, practice of the Coconut Yoga, even by advanced realizers and adepts, not only makes the process easier for aspirants and apprentices, it mysteriously enhances the effectiveness of everybody's work. For an aspirant to discover that an adept is actually willing to be accountable to others for the emotional impact and consequences of his or her speech and action is an amazing, unexpected empowerment. At the same time, it requires the most mature, conscious responsibility of which that aspirant is capable.

Meanwhile, for the adepts, it keeps everybody real and accountable, unable to hide behind a bright shield of realization or transmission. It requires each adept to walk an endless tightrope in mutuality. Being true to his or her total Self includes guarding the integrity of his or her teaching and transmission. Yet the adept must also find ways to surrender emotionally, even when the person being surrendered to cannot fully see that adept's divine identity and essence of grace.

What this kind of receptivity and willingness to be taken down by others produces is a degree of trust that is exceedingly rare. My friends and I have discovered that finding ways to get through the really tight squeezes of reactivity and dissonance empowers and liberates each person. For awakening and awakened beings to be able to find places of real meeting, where previously they found only revulsion and reactivity, produces a faith and trust in Being such as we have never before known.

Eleven

Due Diligence and the Essential Practices of Mutuality in This Way

In traditional cultures, where individuals had an opportunity to choose a spiritual path and a spiritual teacher, the wisest recommendation was always to investigate your options carefully and with discrimination before you made any serious commitment. I have tried to structure the early phases of the path I offer so that you can do exactly that. You and I both, or you and whoever you feel is a candidate to serve you in an adept capacity in this process, should do this.

I've often suggested to people that they approach this investigation with the care that would-be partners to a business contract exercise in what is called, in the commercial world, "due diligence." There it is presumed by both or all potential parties to a contractual arrangement that each one has the obligation and the right to fully investigate each other and all aspects of the contract before signing. Only then will each one have the capacity to enroll himself or herself in the agreement with the fullest possible knowledge beforehand of (a) who his/her partners are, (b) the nature of the agreement itself, in all available detail, and (c) both his/her and the other parties' capacities to follow through on their commitments in a responsible, successful way.

I urge you to practice a sacred form of due diligence in your exploration of the White-Hot Way of Mutuality as a possible vehicle of your own growth, awakening, and ongoing transformation. I strongly recommend that you look carefully into each of the areas mentioned in the previous paragraph before you come to any clear decision. Meanwhile, other adepts serving this work and I will also perform our own due diligence with regard to you.

This is extremely important because the degree of commitment implied in such a partnership is incalculable. In some ways, it is comparable to that of a marriage, and in some ways even exceeds it.

You need to have a clear and complete picture of what you are getting into, as much as that is possible. So do I, or so does whoever will serve you as a primary adept. None of us wants to waste time and energy on something that will not yield fruit, or on something that might be counterproductive, painful, and distressing.

How, then, can you do this due diligence? And what options do you have with regard to finding an adept who can work with you in the manner I am describing?

First, if you seriously want to explore the White-Hot Way of Mutuality, come and spend time not only with me but with other teachers who cooperate with me. You will very likely discover the "click" of heartfelt connection with one or more of us. And this will allow you to begin diving into the process of our approach with good effect.

At the same time, it is important not merely to take a random sampling of how it feels to sit in meditation, converse, and otherwise spend time with me and others here. I urge you to enroll yourself experimentally in the yoga or practice of mutuality with us. This will give you the fullest possible opportunity to clarify for yourself what this Way is and what it is not. This initial, experimental yoga of mutuality takes three forms that also may then be found to characterize the whole process over time. These three forms are Mutual Listening, Mutual Support, and Mutual Commitment.

As the terms imply, these practices are not just for you to take up and try on for size in isolation. They are disciplines of investigation and participation that you may elect to practice in explicit agreement with me and/or other individuals who serve as adepts in this general school of sacred work. That repeated word "mutual" implies that someone else is always doing the work in concert with you. It's not just something you can do by yourself.

Mutual Listening begins with what you are doing right now – reading a book, listening to an audiotape, or even reading an advertisement or brochure about this work, and feeling with your whole being what you are encountering. The listening, in other words, is not merely conceptual. It's not about just getting acclimated to a whole new range of concepts, though that is part of it. To listen in this manner is to receive and apprehend with your whole being an entire communication, which includes words but also springs from and transmits What is the very source of words.

However you begin, at some point you will need to come meet me and/or other adepts associated with me. Whatever events or occasions you choose to meet and get to know us, this is crucial to your listening. The listening becomes mutual, you see, only when you begin to live in direct association with another of the adepts here and/or with me. By "direct association" I mean actual, personal, bodily contact, in the same physical place at the same time, in the waking state, here on Earth. Not that our bodies have to touch, but I must be as aware of and involved in the encounter as you. I specifically do not mean some sort of psychic association on your part, whether through a dream or other means, whereby you feel I have contacted you, or that you have encountered me, but of which I, this man now sitting here typing this essay, have no knowledge in my conscious mind. Direct association requires personal, face to face, human contact. No other form of contact will suffice. At the very least, but even then only temporarily, such contact requires extensive conversation by phone. Sooner or later, the bodies must have their meetings face to face.

You may have to travel to find us, or perhaps one of us will come to where you are, but we do make ourselves available. To me, that is a sacred obligation of the adept's side of the work. You must have frequent and regular access to competent help by an adept who is committed to *you*. If you do not, then your own unique course of Waking Down will not be properly activated and served. I am quite convinced that this is so.

One of the most important occasions for such meetings with me in particular takes place when you are ready to receive a copy of my first major teaching book, *The White-Hot Yoga of the Heart: Divinely Human Self-Realization and Sacred Marriage – A Breakthrough Way for "Westerners."* After you finish a first reading and preliminary study of that text, another occasion will be when you are ready to receive the companion volume, *The Sanctuary of Mutuality: A Waking Maiden Sutra on Embodying the Immortal Nectar of Conscious Love-TRUST.* These large volumes convey the personal Heart-essence of Who I am and many practical details of the White-Hot Way of Mutuality as none of my other books do, or likely will. In the ancient manner, I insist that people come to me personally to receive my full Dharma in each of these books. I require that we enjoy a sacred ceremony of mutual giving and receiving face to face and hand to hand. I speak about this more at the end of this book in "What to Do Next if You Are Interested."

Your practice of listening should involve regular study of my writings and, when available, those of other adept servants of this

Way. I urge people to read at least a little every day, particularly at the beginning when you are first adapting to this process. As I write in *The White-Hot Yoga of the Heart*, the divinely human existence I am living and transmitting is a whole new human sensibility. Many people need real time to even begin to grasp the terminology in such a manner that I can also agree with them, "Yes, sounds like you get that point."

This brings up an important further clarification: the mutuality of our listening requires the adept to listen to the aspirant as intently as the aspirant listens to the adept. The green light that you get from me in Being needs custom coloration for you and you alone. It's not enough for you just to receive a general message that you can dare to grasp the means of your own realization. I have to invoke and evoke YOU in a most personal and particular way. Therefore, whenever you come to spend time with me (I'll speak personally here, and you can extrapolate this to be so for any adept who works with me), I am taking you in, feeling you, sensing all kinds of qualities of your nature – including much of which you are not yet conscious. This is not about psychic knowledge, though sometimes things are revealed in that manner. It is much more a simple and direct being-with-you-*as*-you that is innate to true adept work. And it also includes all kinds of physical, practical, personal experience of and communication with you. We talk with one another, we sit meditatively, we feel how each other is being here. I offer you a glass of water. You take it and drink. Much is transmitted and received in both directions, in ordinary moments of all kinds.

I should mention here that some people don't really land in this work by knowing that life is failing and, thereby, falling into the Rot – at least, not at first. Some people land in the classic traditional manner, by finding themselves in the presence of an adept teacher and feeling profoundly attracted to him or her in a manner that bespeaks the Truth of Being. Thus, the Mutual Listening may first involve a simple encounter that opens the aspirant's heart to the adept's radiant, bodily confidence in Being. On that basis, the aspirant begins to listen to that adept's description of what it is that he or she has realized and why most human beings are not presently enjoying such a free and deeply released condition of existence. In due course, then, the aspirant begins to settle into sensitivity to and as the core wound of confusion and separateness.

It is always wise and honorable to offer some kind of gift in acknowledgment of an adept's presence and instruction or advice, and in support of his or her service to you and others. Thus, I always recommend that people make an offering of some money, along with whatever other gift they may bring, in response to an adept's presence and help. This is a part of the worldwide teacher-student or guru-disciple tradition that I learned under wise instruction. I find it entirely fitting to bring to your attention. People often take, take, take and then wonder why they are having trouble getting, receiving, growing, awakening. They are not grasping an absolute law of nature: to receive, you must give. There is such a secret of growth and wellness of Being in giving! The power inherent in giving fuels the second great practice in the White-Hot Way of Mutuality, which is Mutual Support.

As you become established in the work of Mutual Listening, at some point it will become obvious to you that you are receiving more, and more continuously, than you first may have noticed. If you are working with me or another adept in the White-Hot Way of Mutuality, you may begin to see – if, indeed, it is not obvious to you from the start! – that your adept provides continuous support to you in Being. This support is not merely abstract and transcendent. It is a nurturance that sustains you even bodily, and all the time, twenty-four hours a day. You may feel it most vividly when you are in your adept's physical presence, perhaps especially in meditative gazing, when you and that person are looking deeply into and feeling one another's whole being in silent communion. (I have to note here that you also may *not* feel your adept's support most strongly in such moments of gazing. It's entirely an individual matter; some people take some time to warm to that practice.)

In any case, sooner or later it will dawn on you that your adept partner is always holding, nurturing, and sustaining you in Being. In the Sanskrit traditions of India one of the terms for such support by the adept is "Satsang"– the company of, or association with ("sang"), Being or Truth ("Sat"). My work brings this ancient principle forward in a new way. The secret of the activity of adepts in the White-Hot Way of Mutuality is that they are not only living *with* others in deep psychic intimacy, but, paradoxically, *as* them, in the Onlyness of Being.

When you begin to recognize that this is so, it is good to express your gratitude and also to deepen your receptivity to your adept's blessings by beginning to practice Mutual Support on a more substantial basis. Previously, you may have donated occasional financial offerings, in addition to requested fees for seminars, workshops, books, and the like. Now, if you haven't already been moved to do so, it is altogether to your advantage to provide a continuous reciprocal support for your adept(s) and his/her/their work – a form of sustaining help that you offer regularly in response to the sustaining help that you are receiving.

I recommend the traditional Judaeo-Christian practice of tithing – granting a gift of ten percent of one's income before taxes and before any spending of that income for oneself or others. I can't overemphasize the virtue of this practice. Many of my friends have attested to it. As soon as they started the practice of tithing, their whole lives turned around in many ways. Some of those changes were obviously positive, others tested and tried them, but they felt that it was all auspicious. And they knew it had greatly to do with their entry into the simple but profound discipline of Mutual Support.

When you dare to practice Mutual Support with your adept, the circle of giving and receiving becomes a spiritual cyclotron of true communion. Then the adept's transmission is not only coming to you but being received, ingested, metabolized, and used by you, in all kinds of ways, night and day. Such giving is a practice for which no amount of reading, thinking, meditating, and other subtle activity can compensate. It permits your body to participate deeply in your growing faith and trust that you are indeed receiving an awakening force and instruction in Being. Moreover, it helps you comprehend, bodily, that this force is not coming to you out of the sky. It is coming to you straight through the heart and body and eyes and whole human being of your own adept friend or friends.

Thus, Mutual Support concretizes the yoga of awakening for you. It helps continuously weave all the currents of your own being into the stream of radiant blessing-grace that is any true adept's natural communication to each and every aspirant.

Now I know that for some people such a commitment is extremely difficult. I am also well aware that many people feel they have been exploited and fleeced financially by spiritual teachers and organizations. I try to conduct money-related aspects of my work with integrity and in a spirit of true mutuality. Thus, for instance, I would never permit an aspirant to give to my work, or to me or any other adept, more money than he or she can prudently offer. I have often asked people, "Are you sure you can make this gesture? Are you certain you are not giving too much?" And I always have said that money is not to stand in the way of our working together. I never let people be dissuaded from this Way because they feel they can't afford it.

Even so, in general I observe that people do not suffer so much from giving too much as from not giving enough, or not giving consistently. Therefore, I call everyone to practice Mutual Support in whatever ways are appropriate at each stage of his or her unfolding.

At some phase of your work with me and/or other adepts, the third great practice at the core of the White-Hot Way of Mutuality may come into play for you: Mutual Commitment.

The whole matter of commitment is as difficult and as fraught with perils in sacred intimacy as it is in sexual intimacy. Speaking from experience both as an aspirant and as an adept, I have to say that it is a far more grave and perilous question from the adept's perspective. You should know, then, that I am not casual or blithe about this matter. It is and always will be of huge concern to me, as long as I continue my adept work in any kind of direct relationship with aspirants or apprentice adepts.

When I began teaching, most of the people who approached me had experienced coercion and other forms of manipulation, humiliation, and betrayal in previous sacred relationships. These experiences made for severe breaches of trust with those other teachers and communities. This demographic marker has continued to characterize many, if not most, of those who aspire to use my adept help to their advantage. As a result, and as part of my resolute intention not to superimpose any unnecessary strictures on those who work with me, I have always avoided requiring people to make any overt or formal commitment to me and our process together.

But in reality, this type of sacred intimacy, once mutually embraced, does require some kind of mutual affirmation. It requires commitment. As in sexual intimacy, for most people the stresses that are bound to arise will be so compelling that both partners must be able to count on the other to hold on for the long haul.

At present I have not established any formal process for such commitments with those with whom I work. But I do ask each one to communicate with me privately about this matter. Once an individual finds that he or she is really landing in a sacred connection with me (or with another adept or adepts in our school) and is so moved, then I feel it is both appropriate and necessary for him or her to make a formal affirmation of whatever the nature of his or her commitment actually is. And he or she should do so with any and all adept helpers with whom that commitment is alive.

This process, you see, is quite personal. Your commitment will not touch my heart, or that of any colleague adept friend of mine, if it is only to the Way in some abstract fashion. Rather, we look to establish open, explicit, and entirely mutual commitments and agreements *in relationship* with serious practitioners of our Way.

Each person with whom I have such a mutual commitment presently is in a unique position in relation to me. No one's commitment is exactly the same as anyone else's. Nor is my commitment the same to any two or more of them. Each person's relationship is distinctive, unable to be duplicated, and worthy of its own precise agreements, which that person will almost certainly need to modify over time. Without the container of some form of Mutual Commitment, I have seen it demonstrated that the work of Waking Down can only go so far.

Sometimes people need not only to modify but in effect to withdraw from such a commitment. So it goes, in the sacred life as well as in other intimate personal relations of all kinds. I make room for that. I do not pretend it will not happen. Having had to break my vows of commitment to my guru of over eighteen years, I am not about to suppose that things like that won't happen in my own work. Nonetheless, I do ask that, if and when you find yourself deeply committing to this relationship, you make some kind of formal communication of this commitment to me (or to whomever is serving as your primary adept), and I (or that other) will then need to reciprocate in kind.

The establishment of these three disciplines – Mutual Listening, Mutual Support, and Mutual Commitment – marks a formal conclusion to one's original due diligence with regard to our work. That does not mean that you cease investigating the Way and the nature and workability of our sacred connection. It simply means that the initial exploration has been completed. It means that we have, in effect, entered into a sacred intimacy that we each intend will endure for as long as possible, potentially for the rest of our lives.

These three practices then come to characterize your ongoing love, investigation, and expression of Being, especially in the sacred culture of others similarly occupied. They are the foundations for a truly human culture of awakened freedom and mutuality. They are essential for divinely human life. They are essential forever, as long as and wherever we appear in the mystery of simultaneous Onlyness and Distinctions.

Twelve

Being-Initiation Comes Alive: You Can't Yet See the Sun of Being, but You Start to Feel Its Light and Heat

I can't overestimate the importance of appreciating what we mean by mutuality in this work. But you also need to remember that the quality of mutual vulnerability, accountability, and accessibility that we enter into together depends on each one's reception of the transmission of Being. That reception begins in the earliest moments of your encounter with us, whether through my books or any other means. It initiates a transformation of your whole existence – we might say from the inside out as well as from the outside in. Thus, I refer to that reception of the transmission of Being as "Being-initiation."

In *The White-Hot Yoga of the Heart* I speak of some of the signs that this reception is underway. Often they are not altogether describable. You will simply feel a new hopefulness, a new liveliness, a regeneration of energy that somehow is affecting your whole life. You may sense that it is really coming from (if we may even use directional language) the core or essence of who you are. Nevertheless, you are probably not yet established in stable intuition of the conscious principle or foundation of existence. Thus, to make a natural analogy, you can't yet see the Sun of Being, but you start to feel its light and heat.

Now, that really is an analogy. I am not saying you start to (and I am certainly not saying *you have to*), feel or see a literal, perhaps subtle, light or energy. All such perceptions are at best secondary and usually quite fleeting. Some people have a talent for seeing such things. Others don't. It doesn't matter. Indeed, such a talent can get in the way. I remember counseling one friend who told me all about how she could not help but see auras and the color-intensities of energy in my and others' chakras. It took some painstaking work to get her to realize that those perceptions were really beside the point.

Just so, Being-initiation is not necessarily accompanied by yogic or psychic phenomena of heightened or intensified perception. The light of which I speak is most often simply a lightening up of your whole feeling-tone of existence. I know that to say "you find hope again" may sound simplistic. Perhaps you really haven't lost hope. Well, however simplistic it may sound, I still have to say it! Being-initiation begins with an infusion of new life, new hopefulness, new energy and sense of purpose. Whatever other phenomena may accompany it, these qualities form its simple, central essence.

And these qualities comprise its light.

Then there is also the heat. Another sign that Being-initiation is underway is that your life may feel pretty hot for you at times – as "in the hot seat." Such colloquial phrases often carry great wisdom. The yogic traditions of India speak of the heat of spiritual practice and transformation as "tapas." They are pointing to the energetic and sometimes physically felt heating up of the human organism that occurs when we take on disciplines or enter into fields of force that quicken and intensify our existence. Coming into contact with me and my work tends, I notice, to prompt such quickening and intensification.

What do I mean by that? Well, whether suddenly or gradually, you find you have to deal with your life, your relationships, your work, your health, your family, anything and/or everything in your world in new ways. The pace of changes picks up. Instead of rowing through life at an easy speed, with occasional surges of the current, you find yourself sometimes paddling for dear life through what may appear to be continual rapids. You become more sensitive, more attuned to your own needs and real feelings. And you find that you can't just let things go any more. You have to speak up for yourself more and more. Or you find the world rearranging itself around you. Some friends may appreciate the new intensity and liveliness in you. Others may shy away, even disappear.

You may also go through all kinds of physical shifts and purgings. Your health may get better or worse for no apparent reason. There may be an actual heating of the body, so that you find yourself sweating easily, or just suffering a sometimes uncomfortable heat that appears to be systemic. Problem areas of your body, places where you've had chronic illness, may flare up again, or spontaneously heal, or alternate between the two.

The transmission of Being that you receive from me, or from another adept working in concert with me, works simultaneously from without – we literally transmit something from our bodies to yours – *and from the very Source of your existence.* That Source is not really "within," but then, what another adept or I transmit to you is not really outside you, either. That Source is non-finite, all-encompassing, all-sustaining. It is the Onlyness of Being, of What IS. It is always Being everyone and everything. Yet merely to say so, without realizing its truth, is to miss the vivid reality to which the words are pointing.

When Being-initiation gets underway, even long before you really see the Sun-Consciousness of Being, you start to feel its light and heat.

Welcome to the White-Hot Way of Mutuality! This is when you start to realize that I am not merely using the phrase "White-Hot" for poetic effect.

Thirteen

Re-Parenting Yourself – and Your Adept's Remedial Parenting of You

The great awakening that I am offering and teaching is such a comprehensive transformation of life and consciousness from the very Source of our existence that I call it the second birth. I'll talk more about its special qualities later, but I must, in this chapter, point toward it through discussion of re-parenting and remedial parenting.

In bringing about your second birth, you alone must take the lead role. Another adept or I can ride shotgun with you. To get back to the metaphor of the second birth, we adepts can serve as midwives. Friends and family can provide support and good counsel. But, bizarre as it may sound, you must birth yourself, and therefore you must, as I suggest above, re-parent yourself. This orientation was suggested to me by a man who provided good mentoring during the several months of my own Being-initiation and the total transformation of my existence that occurred thereafter. I have taken that suggestion and developed it extensively in my teachings, especially with regard to self-discipline, effort, will, and grace in the stages of awakening. One of the things I came to see is that Being-initiation, once fully activated, can be considered a kind of second conception. The passage that ensues, one's work toward real awakening, can be seen similarly as a second gestation. And the awakening itself is indeed a second birth.

Once Being-initiation has begun to come alive, it is crucial that you allow yourself to discover the rhythmic pulse of how to re-parent yourself. It may have been important before, but now it becomes critical because your patterns of intentional effort or self-discipline ("fathering") need to be brought into natural effectiveness. And that can only be achieved by permitting a natural balance with patterns of non-effort and self-indulgence, or really self-nurturance, and self-tolerance ("mothering").

74

Many people, and especially those who have spent long years doing aggressively hypermasculine work on themselves, are starving for self-nurturance. And, I am convinced, once a person has begun to show evidence of the beginnings of Being-initiation, in almost every case the next phase of his or her work involves a deep relaxation into self-mothering. You need to permit Being to reveal its own genius and force of intention to awaken in and *as* you. That means that you have to drop just about every activity and habit of self-discipline whereby you have produced, or tried to produce, changes in yourself in the past. This requires a lot of mothering. You have to gently relax the old and acquired modes of modifying behavior, speech, thought, and feeling. By so relaxing, you can just be. You can allow natural impulses to arise and be followed, even if you feel this must be rank self-indulgence, the opposite of any true and truly effective practice toward awakening or liberation.

Admittedly, this is tricky business. A Buddhist practitioner once challenged me, saying that it is absurd and unconscionable to suggest that people just drop self-discipline. "What are you saying?" she asked. "That it's OK for spiritual practitioners just to do whatever they want? You're just going to wind up with a bunch of people drinking, getting promiscuous, and mouthing a bunch of nonsense about how they're all 'awake'!"

My response was that I am not at all proposing that people "just do whatever they want." Rather, I am offering an approach that is built first of all upon the initiation of a new sense, feeling, force, and intensity of Being. Only when this initiation begins to take root in a person's life is it appropriate, I feel, for him or her to seriously consider my teachings about discipline and self-acceptance, or, respectively, self-fathering and self-mothering. But the reason that consideration becomes paramount is that you have to learn a new rhythm of responsive cooperation with the force of Being. Otherwise you will tend to superimpose either your old, hypermasculine habits of self-discipline or your old self-indulgent (but also self-reproachful) habits of indiscipline upon the new event of your Being-initiation. This amounts to constantly throwing static into your own system, or pouring buckets of water onto your just-now-igniting and potentially White-Hot fire.

In most cases, especially for people who have done a lot of work on themselves, what is called for is a preponderance of relaxation. I am not suggesting, however, that you drop all intention and capacity to apply discipline in your life. Rather, I am suggesting that you drop what is often a virtually military regimen of how you have been assuming you must think, act, and be. This almost certainly includes everything you do that you feel is necessary to cultivate freedom or enlightenment. At the very least, I suggest that you question the utility of all your programs for self-change.

Again, let me remind you that these suggestions are not offered to all and sundry, but only to those who find Being-initiation beginning to take root for them and *as* them. When you are beginning to feel the light and the heat of the Sun of Being, it is time, I recommend, to do a lot of relaxing of all your previously acquired and cultivated programs for self-improvement and illumination. Mother yourself. Mother your body. Re-mother your psyche and body with a lot of pampering and what otherwise may seem to you and to others to be self-indulgence. Give your bodily organism a break from any and all regimens that have taken the form of what I've described as superimposed, formulaic seeking.

How, then, does active and even vigorous self-discipline come into play? What is its function in the rhythm of self-mothering and self-fathering? Adi Da used to point to cats as examples of spontaneous, self-energizing participation in life. A cat, he would say, can lie around most of the day, completely relaxed and surrendered into the fundamental energy of its existence. The degree of relaxation a cat exhibits lounging in sunshine far exceeds that which most human beings can ever achieve under any circumstances at all! Nonetheless, when a dog appears nearby, suddenly the cat has all the energy it needs to respond. It is on its feet, hissing or yowling, in an instant. If it has to threaten, it threatens. If attack is required, it attacks. If retreat is necessary, it's gone in no time. But then within moments, as soon as the potential threat disappears from its environment, the cat is again licking its paws and stretching in the sunshine.

So it is with the appearance of self-discipline, or, in the language of this chapter, fathering, in the White-Hot Way of Mutuality. If you are effective in your re-mothering of yourself, then quite naturally you will notice that the current of Being provokes situations and passages in your life that call forth intense, focused self-discipline, or the will to make efforts that are both active and effective. What do I mean by "the current of Being"? Hard to say exactly, except that you notice, once Being-initiation is underway, that your existence itself has a new or much-increased intensity, a liveliness that never stops affecting everything in and around you.

If, like a cat, you spend a lot of time reveling in that current, then when you are moved to *do something,* you find – perhaps initially to your amazement – that you can *really do it,* and even really *do it right the first time.*

What makes these applications of will so fruitful is that they are attuned to the natural rhythms of the awakening being, rather than superimposed and executed in stressful, anxious, conceptually-based ways. When something comes up for you to investigate or do, usually it is just there in front of you in such a way that there is no getting around it. A friend or intimate partner says something – and suddenly a whole realm of your psychological patterning or emotional issues is there before you and won't go away. So you find it natural and inevitable to bear down and feel your way through it all until it is no longer provoking you.

This kind of discipline, you see, relies on the grace of Being itself to be prompted into action. It is not to be laid upon oneself like some kind of heavy yoke on an ox. It is the yoke, the yoga if you will, of Being coming alive and awake as an integrated person, and it finds its own avenues and rhythms of self-expression.

In the early stages of our Way, when people are first overcoming years or lifetimes of hypermasculine self-stricturing, I usually recommend an excess of self-mothering. Afterward you will naturally relearn the self-fathering that is necessary for you, while in the meantime releasing plenty of energy and attention from the often exhausting habits of self-alteration to which you may have become accustomed. As you grow, the alternating cycles of mothering and fathering yourself will become more and more instinctive for you. You will cease to be fundamentally at war with yourself about what you do and do not do for the sake of your growth and transformation. More and more, you'll allow the natural cycles of action and repose, and even positivity and negativity, to reveal themselves in and as your unique personal expression of Being.

That is one side of, again, a curious new appearance of parenting energy and presence in your life as Being-initiation proceeds. The other is the form of parenting that the adept or adepts serving you bring into the picture in their cooperation with you.

When human beings adapt to reception of any kind of living transmission of Spirit or Being-force, they go through natural cycles of change. These cycles correspond to stages of growth from infancy through childhood and adolescence into adulthood, or maturity. This is certainly so in the White-Hot Way of Mutuality. It occurs regardless of the individual's chronological age. Moreover, those who radiate or conduct the transmission find themselves rather automatically being related to as if they were parents of a kind.

There is nothing wrong with any of this. It's all quite inevitable and natural. The trick, on the part of both adepts and aspirants, is to move through the various stages of this remedial parenting with optimal grace, ease, and efficiency.

In the earliest stages of your work in the White-Hot Way, you may very well need, as I have often suggested to others, to tank up on the sacred transmission of Being that you find in the presence of your adept friends. People so often think they are supposed to be self-sufficient in Being from the outset. Well, no such self-sufficiency is truly viable. Those who understand most clearly recognize that we are all interdependent. No one is alone; each and all are supported by each and all. And, beyond that most foundational truth of our relatedness, it is also true that the first stage of receiving a blessing of spiritual grace that you have never received before, is just that: to *receive* it.

Put yourself in the position to drink deep. Why not? My friends and I are committed to finding whatever ways are necessary for each and every truly thirsty person who comes to us to be able to drink deeply, face to face and heart to heart, from one or more adept transmitters. We're committed to finding ways to act as "mother birds" for everybody who comes. Since that is so, give yourself permission to do "baby bird" with us. Open your heart wide, and your whole body, and spend as much time as feels appropriate – which may be more than feels either comfortable or altogether safe – just propping your body up, or even laying it down, in rooms where this transmission is being granted.

There is nothing inappropriate about this dependence. Your body is starved and starving for the nectar of confidence in Being. You can find such nectar only in physical proximity to others who have entered into the integration of the divine and the human that you crave. Your mind, similarly, thirsts for the relief of gaining a liberating understanding of all the hypermasculine propaganda you have swallowed for years, if not millenia. You will not be able to siphon this nectarous nurturance out of the ether, nor merely from books. Your very cells require contact. "Transmission by fleshy proximity," my friend and adept co-worker Van Nguyen calls it. Don't be too proud or too fearful to plug yourself in to it frequently, for as long as you can keep receiving. This is one of the best things you can do.

In contrast to transmissive nurturing, and motherly meeting and holding of individuals in their wounds, pain, and confusion, there are also appropriate and effective ways whereby adepts in this work provide a fathering challenge to aspirants.

This is, of course, a hot topic. People in general love to be mothered and are terrified of being fathered. In this work, as in any other cutting edge enterprise of human transformation, issues often arise with regard to the appropriateness and effectiveness of my and other adepts' more fatherly interactions with aspirants. None of us are trying to tell anyone what to do. None of us are requiring people to be childish. We certainly don't have any such intention, at any rate.

Adepts in this Way provide two basic kinds of fathering challenge to people we work with. Yes, where we come up against limits in your participation in or understanding of Being, and when it appears that you seem intent on defending such limits, we find ways to confront or put a clear light on those limits. Different teachers do this in different ways, and each individual has a variety of styles and modes of serving this kind of encounter. Sometimes a shamanic shout appears to be called for; other times, a more calm, rational conversation. Neither kind of approach is more sacred and auspicious, and sometimes either may prove ineffective, despite the best of intentions.

There is, however, a more fundamental challenge that is going on at all times in your encounter with realized adepts of this process. Our very existence stirs you to be Who YOU are in all Your fullness. Our most ordinary daily interchanges goad you to help you crystallize and integrate all the disparate parts of your nature and, as I write in *The White-Hot Yoga of the Heart*, "come in for a landing." At times our teaching conversations with you will directly focus on this very theme. We'll be invoking and welcoming You in your true and total nature to dare to arrive here in the fullness of your second birth. And we will be magnetizing You, in the silence of our communion in Being, to do just that, with no unnecessary delay. This divine pressure is an ultimate, continuous father-challenge.

At varying stages of the total yoga, you will likely find it necessary and even unavoidable to take breaks from both challenge and receptivity in relation to others. You need these times in order to integrate what you have received, to metabolize it and make it your own. This too is appropriate, an evolutionary benchmark to be celebrated. If your adept or adepts are wise, they will be able to help you identify such times and make optimal use of them.

The remedial parenting performed by adepts in this Way is fraught with the same perils that similar kinds of work face in other fields. Sometimes people can't help but react to those who are helping them. And, in this work we always make it clear that sometimes the adept helpers will react too! Here, we encounter the same kinds of projection and withholding that psychologists and parents also encounter. Oftentimes the early life patterns that people have developed suddenly flare up in relation to their adept. They become convinced that he or she is not really serving them in a pure way, or that he or she is not really or fully awake, or that he or she is in any case totally missing their reality. If people persist and endure through these painful, scary passages, they often find that the crises empower them in all kinds of ways.

As an adept I look to see when and how each person can indeed take steps toward appropriate autonomy and commitment to mutuality. Whenever I see such readiness, I try to find ways to respond to what is present and to evoke yet more self-confidence and responsibility. I look for ways, then, to get people to jump out of the nest and try flying. I try to get each one all the way through the necessary preparatory work, so she or he can actually graduate from this school of awakened conscious embodiment and mutuality, and go on to live it as Being requires. Which, you see, is for each one to discover every day. It is never for me or any other adept – or anyone else – to determine for the awakening or awakened person from outside.

Therefore, as you learn to mother and father yourself in the different phases of this work, you also encounter and, optimally, make good use of the mothering nurturance and fathering challenge of competent adepts.

Fourteen

Greenlighting Yourself as You Are: You Don't Have to Perfect the Body-Mind

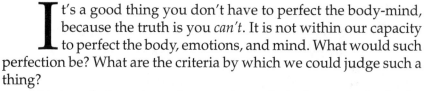

I t's a good thing you don't have to perfect the body-mind, because the truth is you *can't*. It is not within our capacity to perfect the body, emotions, and mind. What would such perfection be? What are the criteria by which we could judge such a thing?

It's true that most people are not exactly trying to perfect body, emotions, and mind. What we must also acknowledge, though, is that even to produce significant changes in them by dint of willful effort is extremely difficult.

Reading this, some people rebel. Others breathe a sigh of relief. The latter are probably better candidates for this particular sacred work. To such people, the news that you can't really perfect or willfully transmute the human organism into some ideal state is more than welcome. This news is an oasis in the desert. It's a transfusion of new blood. It's ultimate food for which they did not know they were searching.

I could go on and on about the theme of this chapter. Over the years of my work with people, I have gone on and on about it many times. You would think that, with all the ideologies of self-acceptance and dharmas of no-seeking that people ingest and then carry like host organisms, it would be natural and easy for them to really get this point. But it's not. Almost never. Those ideologies invariably indicate states of consciousness, mind, emotion, or body that you must first seek to attain, which will then provide sure evidence that you are really ready for freedom from seeking and for safe, ultimate self-acceptance.

They never tell you that it is one hundred percent OK to just stop in your tracks.

They never tell you it's OK to accept yourself as the wretch or weakling you feel or know you are underneath it all.

And even if they do, they don't give you the necessary tools of transmission and other forms of sacred help which allow you to make such a deep acceptance in a manner that liberates you.

Those ideologies and their realizers never give you the green light of Being, and they never, ever encourage you to greenlight your own true and total Self. They may greenlight your true (read: transcendent, immortal, pure and immaculate) ground of conscious identity, your ultimate self. But your total Self, including all your desires, reactions, antisocial and destructive impulses, shadow hatefulness and fear-driven survival instincts? No. You will never get a green light in Being for those aspects of your total Self from the purveyors of hypermasculine ideologies.

In the earliest months and years of my work, I did intensive seminars with individuals who were interested in awakening. I used to tell them, "Take a mug shot"– a police station snapshot of an arrested person – "of your body-mind exactly as it is. This is the one who is going to awaken. Welcome to that wonderfully relieving and terribly distressing reality. Right, you don't have to change all the parts of yourself in order to be able to awaken. You don't have to worry about that any more. Just do exactly what Being requires – which it will reveal to you, don't worry!

"So that's the good news. The bad news is, guess who awakens? You, essentially as you have always known yourself to be! Not some squeaky clean, saintly, superhuman version of you. No – just you, as you are and have been. That's right, awakening does not blissfully relieve you of all the parts of yourself you really hoped would disappear. Welcome home!"

I've memorialized the mug shot metaphor in an essay in *The White-Hot Yoga of the Heart*. Since I develop the idea pretty thoroughly there, I won't go further with it here. I don't need to. This orientation of self-acceptance, of a sustained self-mothering embrace – where you always thought you'd have to just about father yourself to death before becoming worthy of being YOU – is crucial to this Way. Indeed, it's so crucial that we will never be straying far from this point.

When I first conceived and wrote this chapter, I began the title with the phrase, "Accepting Yourself as You Are." But I speak to people frequently about how I give them the green light in Being until they find they are innately doing so for themselves. Even then, and throughout our lives, I think it will always be part of my special gift to others to welcome All of Who you are into fullest incarnate expression. So I wanted to use that term, "greenlighting," in the title.

It occurs to me that greenlighting is probably better for our usage than accepting would be anyway. Accepting implies or at least often connotes a resignation to things as they appear to be. Greenlighting implies giving permission for motion, for change, for a sequence of transformations to occur that allow you to find out who and what you are, and how it is most natural for All of your nature to be revealed and expressed over time. It's a Hollywood word. When producers decide to allow a movie to be made, they greenlight it. At that point, however, all they have is a concept, maybe a script, and perhaps some leads on who will produce, direct, and act in it. All the rest of the moviemaking, including the witnessing of the finished product by others, is ahead of them, a journey unknowable in advance of its own unfoldment.

That being said, perhaps you can understand why I choose the word greenlighting for this particular dynamic of self-acceptance. Greenlight your true and total Self when all you've got for your ultimate divine humanity is an aspiration and, at the moment, empty pockets. Give yourself permission to bring forth the whole, very moving picture of Who you are.

Fifteen

Being-Initiation Comes Awake: Realizing Yourself as Embodied Feeling-Witness Consciousness

F or several chapters I have been introducing the processes and phenomena that may come into play for you as Being-initiation in the White-Hot Way of Mutuality comes alive. For two reasons, I have not talked much about the practices or things you might be doing during this time. First, so much of this stage of the Way is about relaxing effort and doing as little as possible. Second, this is not a book in which I wish to make detailed suggestions for your practice. If you want to hear such advice, you'll have to consult my more explicit practical recommendations, especially in *The White-Hot Yoga of the Heart* and *The Sanctuary of Mutuality*.

Here I have indicated some of the principal experiences and changes you might be going through as this initiation flowers. But I haven't really spoken much of the most fundamental one. What is that? It's the deepening feeling you will be having of becoming yourself. More and more, through all the hard times and the easy ones, through the ups and the downs, you will be landing in and as your obvious and essential self.

At first it won't be clear, perhaps, that this has anything to do with the awakening of transcendent consciousness. Later, though, that will become more clear than the finest glass.

At the same time, you will also be landing in your ordinary human self, your own particular dynamics of body, psyche, and soul.

Let me see if I can be more specific about how all this happens, and offer some indications of your likely concrete experience along the way.

Before sitting down to write this chapter, I spent a morning addressing a group of people who were participating in a workshop we call "The Waking Down Weekend." After a period of meditative silence, including the open-eyed contemplative meeting of each other that we refer to as "gazing," I read aloud the chapter from this book entitled, "The First Birth and Its Now Ending Evolutionary Heyday." When I finished, several people indicated their appreciation. Then one woman, new to our work that weekend, asked for clarification.

The woman – I'll call her "N."– explained that, while she enjoyed the writing, it seemed pretty theoretical to her. And she asked if I could talk about how this kind of transformation actually comes about.

N. further explained that she needed a more practical sense of what could occur for her, and for people in general who carry severe wounds or damage from their experience. As a personal example, she revealed that she had been born in Korea right at the end of the Korean War. Her entire family suffered devastating experiences during and after the war, and she felt herself severely split in her being from that early experience. She had been doing a lot of work with these parts of her psyche, but it was clear to her that much more had to be done. So how, she wondered, could our work serve her healing and reintegration? Could we even deal with such traumas?

By the time she finished her brief account of her early life, several of us who were listening, including me, were in tears – though N. herself was quite composed.

I pointed out to her that the way this process works is, we might say, both from the inside and the outside. The transmission of whole Being-force works simultaneously from awakened and awakening others and from your own Source-nature, which is none other than *the* Source-nature. Thus, I said, that force pushes these and other contents of the deep psyche up to the surface, for us to see and feel and encounter them fully. At the same time, the permitting, welcoming, and honoring participation of others – who have gone or are going through similar openings and revelations – also pulls this traumatic psychic material up, moving us to embody and give voice to what we might otherwise need to protect or hide.

By speaking these pained, difficult parts of ourselves aloud to such deeply sympathetic others – which, I acknowledged, N. was already doing in sharing what she had – we then bring forth the full power of Being to allow the healing to occur. And the salve we feel on or in our psychic and even physical wounds works at the same time as an awakening medicine in consciousness.

After some more conversation along these lines, N. was satisfied with my answer. At this writing it remains to be seen whether the Way of Waking Down will provide a safe harbor for her personally to do that depth of work. In any case, this is how our active communion with one another in this Way stimulates both healing and awakening. I often have to point out to people that the kinds of insight and self-awareness that develop in this Way are different from what you may have gone through before. One of the traps for the grizzled veteran of endless therapy or spiritual transformation is the feeling, "I've already done all that work. I've already seen my early childhood patterns. I already know the ins and outs of exactly how I am damaged, wounded, split, disintegrated. I don't need to look at my deep psychological and emotional issues again. I already know that stuff!"

My reply to such feelings is that a different kind of integration is happening here. This time around the one who is getting to view all that supposedly old stuff of the psyche is the increasingly conscious Being who is awakening and incarnating now as never before.

This is an important distinction, so let me try to clarify it further. Along the continuum of identity, the previous work that people may have done on their "stuff" was generated from the fundamental position, we could say the base camp, of either the material, genetic persona or the individuated soul-nature, the deeper psychic persona. In some cases individuals have also done a certain degree of such work from the position or base camp of the non-individuated, spiritually all-pervading, universal soul, or even that of the non-individuated, transcendent, conscious nature, which is the source or root of both the universal and individual soul-natures. But in each such case, the work is done from a dissociated disposition that is always striving, explicitly or at least implicitly, to affirm and enforce a transcendence of at least the material, genetic persona, if not the individuated soul persona as well.

The very effort to work on one part of yourself from the point of view of another part of yourself reinforces the split between the two parts even while trying to achieve an integration. And most people who make such efforts are often not at all willing to admit that, their expansive spiritual and conscious states notwithstanding, they also really *are* the identity that appears in the context of deep psychological and emotional issues. They won't allow themselves to be reduced to that smallness, that miserable bewilderment and insignificance.

When such individuals become attracted to the White-Hot Way of Mutuality, they begin to fall into the paradox of simultaneity. They begin to know themselves from a new base camp, that of the transcendent, non-individuated Ground of Being-consciousness that is simultaneously identified with and as the material body as never before. This is what Being-initiation leads to in this work. It, Being, *You* as Being, drive into realization of and as the core wound – the simultaneity of infinite and finite nature. As I indicated in the last chapter, this is a most fundamental form of acceptance of the true and total Self. Someone going through this is not trying to make anything happen. He or she is just persisting through and enduring, participating in and cooperating with, a descent into an integration of Being that cannot be prefigured.

Thus, whether an individual is severely damaged in personal, individual ways, or just an ordinary sufferer of the core wound of separateness and confusion, once Being-initiation is alive he or she will naturally gravitate toward integrated awakeness, or conscious embodiment – the second birth. In that process, as a matter of course, that person gets to see whatever aspects of his or her true and total Self need to be seen in order to recognize previous survival patterns from an unprecedented depth of centered, whole-body presence.

Sometimes you won't be feeling that you are entering into any such depth. You'll come talk to me or another adept in the work with a litany of woes and complaints, and we'll say, "Good! Sounds like progress." But you will be feeling the exact opposite. You'll be feeling you're just up against your stuff and now you have no distance, no means to cut through it all, no way to get your arms around it. And we will say it again: "Good! That really is progress!"

Eventually, all of the enlivenment and resurrection of hope and inspiration, along with all the revisitation of primal psychological, emotional, and physical patterns you have developed to survive in this bewilderment of a life, will crystallize into the first real stage of Self-realization. Having spoken of it with a variety of names over the years, I have come to call it realization of "the embodied feeling-witness consciousness."

Before going further, you might ask, "Why? Why, and how, does all of that lead to such a realization?"

I am going to give a key answer to this question in the next chapter. But I can broach that subject now in a basic way.

The answer to the "why" of your question is that Being must come to life first. It must begin to re-animate the living body with hope and inspiration, in order to free sufficient energy and attention for the true and total Self to be able to activate profound Self-awareness. As long as you are depressed, just going along, not activated, not turned on to the prospect of actual realization of Being, your energy is in fact only being sustained at a very low level. Whole Being Self-realization takes juice, it takes life, it takes *spirit*!

The answer to the "how" of your question is that, *in the magnetizing context of truly liberating transmission of Being*, that very enlivenment drives to become fully conscious. In other words, appropriate juxtaposition with other bodies similarly awakening or awake allows you – You – as Being to feel-be-know yourself as transcendent-yet-embodied consciousness. As such, you see that you are naturally, effortlessly witnessing the whole display of soul-nature, mind, body, life, and world as it appears to and in the form of your own organism in each moment. Transmission makes a big difference. So does mutuality. This is how bodies awaken most naturally here. So, at any rate, it appears to me!

I do not find it helpful to speak of the awakening witness consciousness in the traditional Oriental language of exploration of the conscious principle. In almost every case of which I am aware, the classic Oriental schools place supreme value upon a realization of consciousness to the exclusion of phenomena – that is, of everything that appears in and as mind and life and is thereby registered, noticed, or witnessed by consciousness. It's true that some Oriental schools appear not to counsel such exclusion. Nonetheless, if you dig down beneath the surface of their ideologies, you find that their reality belies their affirmations. They carry a taint about life and the possible objects of our experience, both physical and psychic. They promote a sublime prejudice that subtly or not so subtly devalues the conditional, personal, and individual aspects of our personhood while exalting the unconditional, impersonal, and non-individuated ones.

What I mean by the embodied feeling-witness consciousness is a crystallization of the reality of the inescapable paradox of being alive – the paradox of being infinite and finite at the same time. Suddenly the fact of your infinite, or non-finite, primordial conscious nature becomes as obvious to you as the fact of your finite, ever-changing material nature. Yet your realization of your identity *as* that indefinable conscious principle does not set you at any overwhelming distance from the reality of your identity as the finite, mortal, local human person. You land simultaneously in your conscious nature and your bodily, human personhood. That landing, whether sudden or gradual, is an arriving at once into your own unique personal life and into the unconditioned, unknowable Ground of Being that is consciousness. You fall or drop into an unspeakable, yet ever so ordinary, permission to the conscious, psychic, and material parts of your being to be what they are without any further fundamental dissociation from one another.

Perhaps this may sound like ultimate realization of the Onlyness of all consciousness and all phenomena. No – that's not so. The person established in this stage of awakening has arrived into a new depth of incarnation or embodiment, yes. But the absolute non-difference between consciousness and phenomena has not yet become obvious. Yet it is also true that, in the awakening of the embodied feeling-witness consciousness, a certain degree of reconciliation or integration of the disparate parts of the whole being has occurred.

This preliminary realization turns the key in your ignition in a new way. Now another kind of journey commences. Whereas in the earlier stages, when Being-initiation was coming alive, you continued to suffer a primal confusion or split in your identity, now something about that dis-ease or disintegration has dissolved. I remember that when this stage opened up for me, a couple of phrases came to mind that named the new quality: singularity of Being and confidence in Being. Difficulties still arise, and the ultimate connection between conscious identity and relatedness to all others and things remains unclear. But you find yourself moving through the difficulties in a different manner than was ever possible before. And you have refreshed, vigorous, effective drive to examine that ultimate connection until clarity appears.

This fall into the Heart-Ground of Being and Consciousness is an immense breakthrough in your evolutionary journey. Now, Being-initiation has come awake in a manner that you will find yourself less and less able to deny. And though there are many things that you and your adept(s) can and will have done to expedite this shift in your Being, most fundamental to making it possible is your simply daring to grasp the means of realizing and expressing Who you are. Awakening as the embodied feeling-witness consciousness is the first stage of divinely human participation in life. I have compared it to conception – this time leading to the second birth.

It's important, in this definitive overview of the White-Hot Way of Mutuality, to place some of this technical language in clear sequences and juxtapositions. Your Being-initiation first gets underway when it begins to come alive. Though I first used that language in Chapter Twelve, I have been speaking of that stage of the Way in more and more detail since defining transmission and the adept's job in Chapter Nine. However, it is only at the phase I am describing in this chapter, the realization of the embodied witness-consciousness, that your Being-initiation comes fully awake. And it is only at this stage that you enjoy what I refer to as fully functional Being-initiation. This degree of awakeness, then, is what I call the second conception.

Let me say a few things about this quality of Being-initiation that will help ground it for you in practical life-terms.

The revelation of the witness-consciousness as this whole-being embodiment is a realization, not just a temporary opening, samadhi, or satori. But your experience of its qualities begins shifting very soon after the realization is established – such that you may think that you have lost it. There is a very good evolutionary reason for this, which I will address in the next chapter. Now I just want to point out that there is a dimension of this shift in Being that remains continuously established ever afterward. Fully functional Being-initiation is a new stage of life, a categorical transition in the fundamental quality of your conscious presence and participation in the world. Yet, bizarrely enough, you can feel as if you are not really holding the transition. You can feel as if you are helplessly gravitating back into your ordinary confusion and separateness, perhaps as you have many times in the past.

The reason this is so is that you will tend, initially, to identify the essence of the realization with certain qualities of its breakthrough appearance in your body, mind, and deep psyche or soul-nature. Often the first flush of this stage of awakening is accompanied by a sense of fathomless depth of consciousness, of infinite spaciousness in Being, of clarity, imperturbability, serenity, ease, and grace. However, none of these qualities of psyche or body in and of themselves, nor all of them together, define the realization. Rather, this awakening constitutes a shift in what I have called your center of identity-gravity. You begin to discover that you are fundamentally, and indeed effortlessly, based in a different place or quality of your total nature.

This shift is nothing less than a falling into Heart-Consciousness as your new base of identity-gravity. And this particular "base camp" is fallen out the bottom of the cosmos. In other words, it is not just some precious little intuition that consciousness is the Ground of Being. One who has passed into this disposition is fundamentally located outside or transcendental to all of cosmic and personal Nature. He or she is standing in and as the dimensionless dimension, the featureless feature of existence, the non-thing that registers, notices, effortlessly apprehends but is always untouched by absolutely all things and beings that display themselves before it.

The conscious nature that you are now living as and also embodying is realized or known to be transcendental to absolutely everything conditional or phenomenal. The world, others, things, objects, events – including thoughts, feelings, sensations, reveries, impulses, dreams, the sense of your basic daily identity, and all the subconscious and unconscious rumblings and subliminal movements of which you are sometimes aware – all of these, and every other possible thing, event, or process that you can experience as an object to your simplest and most essential subjective nature, is part of the conditioned cosmos that you, as consciousness, are now transcending. This doesn't just include local, familiar beings, things, and events. It includes every heavenly and hellish kind of experience you could possibly have. It even includes perception of and union with God, the Truth, the divine Reality. Whatever such a Thing, Being, or Event may be for you, this feeling-conscious nature is witnessing, or registering, even it and your gnosis of or communion with it.

You realize this to be so, but the realization is not in the mind and body that you are now transcending. That mind and body, including the deep soul-nature or root of the psyche, now must go through a basic adaptation to the new ground of their Being. That ground, paradoxically, is also absolutely free of all this psycho-physical personhood and en-world-edness – even while, in some sense, it is right up against it all, exposed to it.

Thus, fully functional Being-initiation – this awakening into embodiment as the feeling-witness consciousness – instigates a new stage of living. It is, again, the second great conception in the grand evolutionary journey of your existence. I venture to propose that, whatever great realizations may have occurred in this or previous lifetimes, this second conception, in its precise details, is a new event for you, as it is for each one who passes into it.

What then comes after conception is, of course, gestation.

Sixteen

The Second Gestation: Oscillations, Governing Sentimentalities, Quantum Vision, and the Genius of Awakening Being

One of the reasons I like the birth analogy is that, if only the conditions are met to ensure conception and a viable pregnancy, then the events I am describing take place with an almost ruthless biological inevitability. More to the point, I regard these events to be quite as natural to the human animal as getting born in the first place – *if*, and it is of course a big "if," the necessary conditions are met to make them possible.

I propose that this kind of transformation and awakening cannot help but occur if people are ready for it and dare to grasp the means. And, once again, I feel that many people are now ready and many, many, many others soon will be. Many, as in hundreds, thousands, even millions, not merely ones or twos or even dozens. Soon, as in months, years, at most decades, not centuries or millenia. It is such a natural unfolding, so custom-made for each individual – I never cease to marvel at how this works. I could be wrong in my predictions, but I am confident in the genius of awakening and awakened Being.

Take, for present example, this second gestation.

I have already alluded to some of the phenomena people experience going through this stage of realization. The dawning of the feeling-witness consciousness in embodiment is often a great initiatory bath in the sublimity of Self-realizing existence. It's not uncommon for people to feel a great ease, lightness, and grace pervading their lives for days or even weeks. But, sooner or later, and often to their horror, they begin to feel a return to the conditions of ordinariness. Actually, ordinariness in and of itself doesn't really disturb them. What disturbs them is the appearance of patterns that (a) they thought they had seen clearly long before and long since outgrown, (b) they assumed that embodied witness realization would automatically make them immune to forever, and/or (c) they never even knew they had.

I call these appearances "oscillations." I have written about oscillations at some length in *The White-Hot Yoga of the Heart.* In this book I just want to make a few germane points.

First, *the embodied feeling-witness realization is not an end in itself.* Am I repeating myself? Didn't I just say this in the last chapter? Yes, I did. But it bears repeating. Indeed, it winds up bearing repeating almost every time I encounter someone who has just gone through this stage of awakening. And that is not because people are dumb or because they aren't listening. It's because, after the initial bath of Self-grace, when their old patterns re-emerge, even though they have read and heard me speak about this dozens of times, people tend to freak out a little bit. They *think* they have lost or are losing their awakening into and as witness consciousness. It's completely natural to think so. Indeed, that thought is the intelligent, necessary discrimination to make at this particular moment of the evolution of Being.

In our real, bio-spiritual unfoldment, losing awakening is not what's actually happening at this point. No. The more transparent, spacious, and gracious qualities of this awakening are not meant to last, any more than, in the first birth, the mother's and father's ecstatic experience at the time of conception is destined to persist. What has to happen next is that you need to see many of the most characteristic patterns of mind and life that you have put together in your whole first birth adventure. At times you'll probably even need to feel as if you were drowning in them.

Now why, you may ask, do you need to see and feel such things?

Because it is the genius of awakening Being to shed old skins in order to make room for a new, second life. Once true and total Being clearly gets the green light to realize and express itself fully, it begins to overhaul the whole organism, the whole circuitry and wiring of life-patterns. The only way it can do so is by revisiting all of its most crucial dynamisms, especially the ones that were cobbled together in instinctual reaction to the wounds of relatedness and the bewilderment of identity, whether early or relatively lately in life. Thus, awakening Being does not really want to avoid all those old and disturbing patterns. Whatever your mind may think, however you may feel about these matters emotionally, you, You, Being, must bring as much of all that patterning up for revisitation as is necessary.

What, then, determines what is and is not necessary?

The answer to this question is breathtakingly simple in principle. I first heard it articulated by Adi Da. Happily, in my own realization and now that of quite a number of others, I have seen this ideal principle demonstrated again and again by Being in the active working out of Self-realization. This is the big secret, the immutable law of the genius of our nature:

Once Being greenlights itself for the second birth, or divinely human awakening, it prompts every necessary experience, and only those truly necessary, for it to liberate sufficient energy and attention from old, first birth patterns. This liberated energy and attention then are spontaneously employed to allow the conscious nature to stand in natural, non-separate Onlyness with all the manifest phenomena of life and mind, world and soul.

I can't overstate the grace and economy of this process. If Being is allowed to conduct its own love, investigation, and expression in and as each individual, then that person will go through just exactly what he or she needs to, nothing more nor less, in order for consciousness to realize its infinite freedom in the finite limits of embodiment, without fundamental confusion or separation. I have seen it happen again and again. It is most impressive.

You may say, "Well, sure, but it's pretty easy for you to decree that what any individual has gone through is just what was necessary, no more and no less, for him or her to awaken. Twenty-twenty hindsight – but who can really say? Who can truly know?"

To which I can only reply, yes, on some level this is Monday morning quarterbacking. Still, if you will talk to the individuals who have advanced in the White-Hot Way of Mutuality to this degree, I think you will find that they convey their own amazement at this economy and elegance of awakening Being. They too, and each in his or her own way, sense the streamlining of their whole existence in ways that they never could have come up with through their previous orientations.

What people go through, of course, is totally fingerprint unique in each person's life. Because there is almost no standard practice in this Way, no cultural mode of life to which everyone must conform, people go through their awakenings in the midst of their own experiences and their distinctive structures of relationship. Everyone has his or her own challenges and struggles. Everyone has his or her own joys and victories. We all tend to delight in the differences and marvel at the personal genius and trials of each individual other.

Even so, there certainly are some characteristic qualities to the process that I have observed to be pretty universal. I mentioned oscillations above – oscillations, you see, out of the confidence in Being that our kind of witness realization prompts, and back into patterns of separateness and confusion that disturb, thwart, and even appear to sabotage what you have already clarified. In addition to such apparent regressions, there are two other characteristic features of the second gestation: recognition of these patterns as governing sentimentalities, and the understanding and participation in such recognition through what I call quantum vision.

Governing sentimentalities are what you oscillate back into when you appear to lose your feeling-witness awakeness and become absorbed again in patterns of mind and psyche. I use that word "appear" because, over time, it will become clear to you that you only seemed to lose your new ground in Being. You did not really do so at any moment. But the appearance is, nonetheless, compelling each time.

Why?

When these oscillations occur, you feel rather helpless. You suffer a compulsive, reflexive reactivity. You instinctually try to control it but quickly discover that you really can't. What absorbs your attention and seems to diminish or destroy your newly discovered foundation of freedom functions like a kind, or many kinds, of addiction for you. That's why I respectfully call these things governing sentimentalities. They are preferences, prejudices, characteristic ways of feeling and thinking in response to specific qualities of experience or different kinds of events. All of them exert a controlling influence upon your whole subjective mind-force. Yet further investigation reveals that they are *not* direct responses to actual, present realities.

Even your most feared and hated addictive habits of mind and emotional reactivity – say, for example, your tendency to feel dismissed, abandoned, and worthless – are eventually found to exert a nostalgic, almost wistful magic on the mind. Yes: you discover that you actually have a sentimental attachment to these deep dark qualities of your sense of who you are. Whatever reality these feeling patterns may have had in the early stages of becoming established, you now begin to notice, usually after a few oscillations back into their psychic zones, that they are unreal. They are sentimental moods, not really intelligent responses at all. Yet they have governed your participation in reality.

What changes the quality of your participation, then? Not attempts to muscle a transformation into place. You can't really do that any more. Your embodiment as the feeling-witness consciousness renders your encounter of all the qualities of life and mind much more stark. You no longer seriously feel that you can really even try to decide to do something about these mind-addictions you are now revisiting.

Instead, if you simply persist and endure in the whole yoga of our work together, you notice another principle coming into effective play. It is the principle of consciousness itself. And it functions, with regard to all such governing sentimentalities, as what I call quantum vision.

The quantum understanding of physical reality holds that the very process of observation alters the nature and even location of that which is observed. Indeed, it suggests that, at subatomic levels, the very act of seeing alters the whole field of seer and seen. As you deepen in your new ground or center of identity in consciousness, which is the embodied feeling-witness starkly present to mind, life, and relationships, you begin to notice a quantum event taking place in you, *as you*. You see that what changes the quality of governing sentimentalities in your life is the very act of your felt observation of them by, in, and as consciousness. The sheer, raw fact of your noticing these trends of psyche and mind, even while feeling helplessly controlled by them, subtly shifts the balance of power, we might say, in your favor.

During the second gestation, what makes the great difference is not that the sentimentalities, attitudes, prejudices, and addictive patterns disappear, or even that they significantly change. Nothing of the sort may occur. And even if it does, that in itself is not the most important change. What makes the great difference, rather, is that *you notice that you are no longer exclusively identified with these patterns the way you used to be.* You see that in some ways you experience them with even greater intensity than before. Yet, curiously enough, you also now enjoy a kind of distance, a humor, a perspective with regard to them.

No matter how many enlightenment experiences or flashes of

transcendence you ever enjoyed in the past, now, in your embodiment of the witnessing nature of consciousness, you find a self-sustaining power in your freedom that you never knew before. It is the most elusive thing, hard to put your finger on. After all, the freedom is not made out of distance from what you are experiencing. You're *in* your stuff like never before – and yet, somehow, you are also not ground up in it as you used to be.

Such is quantum vision. It is the genius of awakening Being to expose to the awakening conscious nature all necessary governing sentimentalities. The raw event of the exposure guarantees that the conscious nature will recognize the subjective patterning of the psyche and all the stubborn habits of mind, body, and relationship with ever-increasing clarity over time.

The recognition, you see, is inevitable if the exposure simply occurs. Therefore, awakening Being must oscillate into such exposures again and again. Only in that manner can it, and does it, liberate energy and attention from exclusive absorption in those patterns. Thus liberated through quantum vision, that energy and attention is then freed in service to the awakening of whole Being conscious embodiment, or the second birth, the entry into divinely human existence.

I hope this makes sense to you. I realize I am stuffing a lot of new language into a small space here! But if you begin to get the thread of what I am saying, you will begin also to sense a great relief and new hope. Being really wants to awaken in, as, and through *you*. You, indeed, are that one and only Being. You always have been. You always will be. Now, however, at last – if you are so inclined, and so "Hungry"– there is a direct way for You, as Being, to accomplish this total greenlighting of your incarnation, as never before. You don't have to change, alter, conquer, or overcome your negative, dark, stubborn qualities and habits. A few alterations may reveal themselves to be necessary, yes. But working on your qualities is not what makes this so effective. It is recognition, quantum vision, that makes this Way so effective. And you don't have to do much of anything to try to get that quantum vision activated in and as you. Mostly, you just have to persist and endure in this alchemical relaxation into being who you are in mutuality with others of us – including one or two adept friends working with you closely – who are living in the same manner themselves.

One of the amazing things about this awakening is that it is all so natural and inevitable, so, yes, *biologically unstoppable*. If we work together to ensure that the conditions for a successful gestation are met, a successful and healthy second birth is virtually guaranteed.

To me, this is just astonishing, wonderful news. Perhaps you're not convinced yet. I suppose you can't really be convinced until the reality of it all is undeniably your own, no longer merely a theoretical proposition I am making to you. Well, I respect that need – so read on, and let's continue.

Seventeen

The Potential Blazes of Consciousness

Much can and must be said about how the embodied feeling-witness consciousness accomplishes its work through quantum vision of the total human person alive in its relationships. You'll find this discussed in both *The White-Hot Yoga of the Heart* and *The Sanctuary of Mutuality*.

Here I'm going to skip ahead to what happens next – after making one particular point.

That point is this: you must come to enjoy unshakable confidence in the absolute freedom of your own conscious nature. I do mean *absolute freedom*.

To realize the core wound at the evolutionary stage of the feeling-witness awake in conscious embodiment is, I again propose, an advance upon the old, dissociated qualities of witness realization. In this realization, one continues to endure and enjoy the heart of our human paradox of simultaneous limitlessness and limitedness. But the continued enduring of, and even the whole-hearted participation in, the limits of existence in bodily form must not fundamentally compromise or dilute the absoluteness of one's freedom in and as consciousness.

The feeling-witness consciousness stands absolutely free *of* the body, even the soul-nature, and all the activities, events, processes, and relations of the total individuated personality. At the same time – the heartbreaking paradox – it stands free *as* that very manifest one, in its, his or her, every detail. This simultaneity must be realized. This must be known. This must be enjoyed, otherwise the Heart-Ground of one's realization of Being remains attenuated and unclear. I am not talking about some slick intellection about consciousness combined with a life of karmic indiscipline, or self-indulgence. I am talking about a landing in conscious freedom and embodied ordinariness in a manner that spontaneously alters the whole future course of one's life.

If this very marvel of realization opens up for you, as you, then you will likely spend some time cycling through the quantum work of witnessing that I described in the last chapter. At some point, however, that work will have completed its necessary initial tasks.

You may not know this yet, of course. You may think you still really need to be focused on participating in the ongoing revelation brought about by various oscillations into governing sentimentalities and such, old and new. But at a deeper or more central place than that of your thinking, interpreting mind, Being at some point begins to abide in such an increasingly strong confidence that it cannot help but inherently witness whatever phenomena appear to consciousness. Once that confidence begins to emerge – and, again, you may not be in a position to know with mental certainty that this is even so – then the conscious nature embarks upon a more profound adventure still.

At first, you see, it is amazing to the newly awakening consciousness just to find itself more or less stably alive and awake in bodily incarnation. I don't know how to describe this to you. I can say that this amazement appears frequently. I have heard exclamations from my friends that confirm this observation, which first arose for me during my own period of gestating into the second birth.

You need some time to do the work of quantum witnessing, yes. And that work does free up more energy and attention from compulsive addiction to governing sentimentalities, yes. But in the most practical terms, you just have to prove to yourself that you really are that free conscious nature awakening. It's too good to be true, too outlandish to be believed, too ordinary to be sufficient – yet, it is all of this, and more, and less. It's a mystery, and it takes time to adapt. You take your sweet time, so to speak. You allow the recognition again and again that you are indeed inherently standing free as that which silently, effortlessly notices, registers, or witnesses the appearance, persistence, change, and disappearance of all the manifold phenomena of your living.

By the way, on this point, you do not have to work to bring the feeling-witness consciousness to active responsibility in dreams and sleep, as well as the waking state. Not to enter the second birth as I understand it, you don't. You do not have to maintain some military regimen of vigilance to make sure you don't lose that quality of consciousness. No. Remember what I proposed in the last chapter? You *need* to lose the crystalline awakeness of the witness repeatedly, in order to expose your true and total conscious Being to the muck and the vicissitudes of mind, psyche, and limited personhood.

Well, when the initial period of such witnessing and oscillating has essentially been fulfilled, quite naturally another enterprise may open up in consciousness. You may not be aware of it as such. I certainly was not aware of the shift when it occurred for me. Indeed, it was not until several years later that I happened to ascertain it. Again, it takes time for conscious Being to fully cognize the whole event and all the benchmarks of its own incarnate realization.

What is that other enterprise? Before I describe it, I must also say that it is only potential. Not everyone will go through something like it, I believe. Indeed, the evidence of my friends suggests that many people, maybe even most, will not. Even so, my very speaking of it will help you crystallize its benefits in your own process in due course, whether or not you pass through it as a whole phase of your own yoga.

The next enterprise involves a blazing forth of consciousness in Self-awareness. Suddenly, or gradually, the conscious principle ceases to be concerned with or focused attentively toward its own witnessing activity. That is just going on without intention or effort, like the inherent and inevitable machine that it is in Being. Therefore, the conscious principle is free to do something else. "Do," so to speak – consciousness doesn't really do anything. These passages are so sheer, so difficult to render with any accuracy at all in speech. Nonetheless, there is a kind of activity, a form of intention and consequent motion, that proceeds in the conscious nature itself.

At this point, the conscious principle simply begins to revel in and examine its own mysterious presence. It ceases to maintain any but the most necessary regard for what it is otherwise and always, inherently witnessing. This reveling may be accompanied, as it was for me, by an intensification of one's awareness of the qualities of consciousness – its self-luminosity, its self-existingness, its inseparability from Being or existence altogether, its inherent wellness, freedom, delight, and happiness. There was a particular incident when this occurred for me. I remember feeling with vivid clarity that it was as if body, mind, and all the associated phenomena of the whole world had been blasted to the corners of the room of Being. There I sat, or stood, in the center of my world, quite awake to my natural witnessing of everyone and everything, yet marveling at the pillar of fire of conscious Being that I was and am in the midst of all. This was not "Cosmic Consciousness," by the way. It was not a vision of the entire universe and all its workings. It was me being aware of the room in my apartment and the world of my body, mind, life, and relationships – and on fire with the being of Being!

Afterward, the quality of blazing intensity diminished in my daily living. But the natural reveling in and as consciousness itself and the free confidence in Being who I am, without concern to reinforce the witness-function – these characterized my entire passage thereafter, until my second birth a short time later.

Not everyone who has awakened into the second birth through working with me has had such a dramatic opening or transition beyond the witnessing stage. Most can point to some kind of shift or transition; some cannot, until the second birth itself. Therefore, I point to this blazing forth of the conscious nature as a potential, but not at all a necessary event in your own journey.

There is another kind of blaze that may occur. Its nature and indeed its very possibility shed some light on how indeterminable all this is for us. My feeling, you see, is that we are at such an early, pioneering stage of registering these transitions that we are in no way equipped to make absolute statements about what can, will, or will not happen along the way for any individual. Certain general statements can be made, but I know well that they too will be vulnerable to further refinement as we go.

That other blaze-forth is what I call "the White Heat" of Conscious Embodiment. It comprises the glitch factor, Element X, in our whole consideration of the sequence of events leading to and beyond the second birth awakening. Why? Because, in the normal evolutionary course of events, it comes well after the second birth awakening. But it may manifest as an initiatory burn-through even well *before* that awakening – thus quickening it and, among other things, perhaps even completely wrecking, disproving, and upending the clever, logical sequence of conscious transitions that I am presenting in these chapters!

What occurs in this conflagration of Being is something like this. The conscious nature and all material and other manifest phenomena are instantaneously revealed to be absolutely non-separate – to a much greater degree than even occurs in the recognition of non-separateness that marks the second birth. The Onlyness of Being flashes, at least for a moment, into an intensity of such radiant force and sublimity that one ceases to be aware of any and all conditional appearances within that infinite and all-pervading Blast.

Because it is of the nature of consciousness, even to use a word like "blast" may seem overly dramatic and phenomenal. I don't know how to not make much of this event. It might be compared to the stage of the life of a star when it becomes a supernova. After radiating brilliantly for eons, suddenly the star flares up and explodes into a much brighter and larger immensity.

That image gives a picture of something like what this instantaneous White-Hot blazing of Being entails. But only a picture. My friends have sometimes complained that I don't really give a better picture. In all the teachings of which I am aware, only Adi Da has suggested that something along these lines is the destination of our evolution. He speaks of "Outshining" and, ultimately, "Divine Translation." It was in Adi Da's presence that I received an initiatory glimpse of this consummate dimension of reality. Later, after leaving his work and awakening, I brought it forth in my own autonomous explorations of Being. The reason I bring his work up here is to make this point: the divine adept whom I regard to have made the first revelation along these lines also proposes that this kind of passage is inherently unknowable and indescribable.

Once this White-Hot intensity shines forth, even if only for an instant, it can tend to short-circuit and alter the otherwise natural patterning of how the second birth and its aftermath appear. I have seen in at least one case, that of my friend and adept colleague Rene Hansen, how this White-Hot intensity, contacted at the outset of one's practice in the White-Hot Way of Mutuality, appears to have economized the necessary period of witnessing. It also appears to have rendered that other, less all-consuming blaze of conscious Self-contemplation unnecessary or indistinguishable from the witnessing phase of the second gestation.

Let my adept friends and me know how all these phases and qualities of awakening do or do not show up for you. We'll be interested to hear about all this.

Eighteen

Your Second Birth Awakening: The Seamlessness of Divinely Human Conscious Embodiment

Y ou may or may not pass through a blaze-like shining forth of consciousness to and as itself. You may, instead, simply find your confidence in Being deepening while you witness the endless display of changes that make up your life and mind from day to day. You may even suffer what appears to be an endless oscillation into the swamp of deep psychological and emotional issues, so that you can barely even remember the simplicity of feeling-witnessing. I have one friend, my co-worker Sandra Glickman, who awakened in just such a manner. Regardless, one way or another, sooner or later you will simply arrive in the sudden and stark ease of divinely human realization of Being.

The essence of this transition is that the conscious nature now, and in most cases quite suddenly, recognizes that there is no separation whatsoever between itself and the All-Consciousness that is Being – nor any such separation between it and any and all phenomena in the world of appearing things, others, and events.

In a word, Being knows itself to be not just One but Only – and at once inclusive of everyone and everything, yet completely free of any dependence upon any phenomenon at all, even your own body, soul-nature, or sense of "me" or "I."

The immediate descriptive term that leaped to my mind the moment this realization dawned in me was "seamless." I saw that the entire world of appearances and my own consciousness and whatever the Great Consciousness of All IS are entirely continuous. Suddenly it was obvious that there are no seams to be found in reality anywhere, under any conditions whatsoever. Yet apparent separations remain. All the distinctions I found in life and mind before persisted, some with even greater tenacity. But I ceased to be fundamentally at war with What IS. All of it. Not just with the great overriding divine reality, but with the ordinary aspects of daily human living, breathing, eating, sleeping, thinking, desiring, acting, resting, speaking, relating, arguing, suffering, hurting, loving, you name it: all of it.

When the feeling-witness realization had broken through, in my case a couple of months before, I had marveled at the sudden confidence in Being that began to characterize my very core. But I shuttled through a variety of oscillations until this crossing of the great divide of fundamental confusion and separateness took place. From that point on (it was early December, 1992), there has always persisted this fundamental Wellness and Integrity of Being. No matter what else has taken place, no matter what states of mind, psyche, and soul-illumination or darkness I have suffered or enjoyed, I have always been established in and as the Onlyness of All that Is. And I have been That, I Am That, without the slightest need to differentiate it in any way from my human ordinariness. That unremarkable humanity has continued to display itself with, if anything, stubborn expression of its natural weaknesses, liabilities, faults, and shortcomings.

I will be talking about this second birth awakening in many ways throughout this book and throughout all my other writings. I don't feel the need to make this chapter an exhaustive reconnoitering of what it entails, as if such a thing were even possible. But I do want to point to a few prominent characteristics. Keep in mind, please, that I am not speaking here of attitudes of the mind or psyche or body. I am speaking of the nature of the realized, incarnating consciousness.

First, this awakeness is *self-validating*. Your second birth communicates itself as a greater and greater confidence in itself, *as* you. Not merely in you, nor merely at the Source of all the rest of you, but *as* you in your basic entirety. It may be helpful for others to confirm that they feel you have entered into such Self-confidence. But you don't really need validation from anyone. Compared to the confusion and anxiety of your previous modes of being, this sublime condition is the very archetype of Self-assurance. You just can't fundamentally help but Be Who You Are, all of it, all of you, and that's that. Yes, there will be moments of doubt in the mind – you burn through them and emerge more confident than ever before. Even all the crises and ordeals that you move through in your second life prove to you more and more conclusively that, at heart, you are a radically changed human being. It's not only that no one else has to tell you so. No one else *can* tell you so. This second birth realization is self-validating.

Also, the inherent nature of the realized state is such that it is not actively doing anything, even including, emanating, manifesting, permeating, or pervading all things and beings. Rather, it is by nature just Being whatever IS. This is an important distinction. You will see its utility over time in your own realized presence and participation in life.

In a way, the transition into the second birth is analogous to a wave's realization of its absolute identification with the entire ocean – while still remaining and being just exactly the wave that it is. In the Epilogue of this book, I write, "Abide, yourself, as the Ocean of all Being, inherently non-separate from and indeed indissolubly identical to one and all, and All. And 'wave' that Oceanic Identity into the fullest and most creative possible expression in your unique personal life."

Though many traditional teachings and adepts speak of awakening in terms that sound very much like this, I regard the great modern master Adi Da to be the original evolutionary progenitor of this precise realization of the nature of Being. I differ with Adi Da in many respects, especially on the manner of participation in life and relationship that any individual might build upon such realization. He uses his own language, almost none of which I have found suitable for expressing my particular orientation. Nonetheless, with regard to the realization that I describe as conscious embodiment or the second birth, his writings on what he calls "the seventh stage of life" are an unprecedented articulation.

Some years ago, in one of his early books, *The Paradox of Instruction*, Adi Da offered a profound analogy that I have used many times in my own work. There he pointed out that the event of realization is not like expansion from a point to some infinite beyond, but rather like the way a blown-up balloon, when punctured, suddenly equalizes with all space. The moment of my own transition into the second birth had that exact quality. Suddenly a sense of pressure that had always driven me, like a pent-up force within, was instantly equalized with all space. Until that moment I had not even been able to know that such a pressure existed. And, once it was released, I sensed immediately that it could never return.

These, then, are some of the qualities of the second birth that you also may notice. This realization is so extraordinary that you can never, ever fully comprehend it, or your Self, thereafter. Yet it is so ordinary that at times you can't find any realization to point to at all. Indeed, this is one of its paradoxical hallmarks. True realization of the wholeness and singularity of Being does not stand out from ordinary human existence. You don't have a state to point to. There is no transcendence of your continuing human presence and ways of living, as you may have previously felt and known transcendence: a standing apart, an alternative or altered state, a subtle difference between yourself and everything and everyone being transcended. Now, in contrast, you are right here, you are not apart, you are not fundamentally beyond. Yet, in this realization, the transcendence is absolute, incontrovertible, immense, unimpeachable. It is not a liberation from life and this world. It is liberation *into* life in and *as* this world and all conditional reality, simultaneous with the absolutely unconditional reality. Go figure!

And it is so *obvious*. When it dawns upon you, as you, you won't be jumping for joy, weeping with the all-obliterating Beauty of it all. Much more likely, you'll simply notice a sudden shift in Being that you immediately sense will be irrevocable. And you'll think, or at any rate I did, "Oh, *right*. This is what I was seeking all those years, all those lifetimes! How incredibly simple. How blithering obvious. Of *course!*"

The second birth is a most summary arrival into your own life in its totality. It opens you up into a marvelous stage of human evolution, in which you are always simultaneously living your God-consciousness and your animal instincts, and you find less and less excuse to make divisions between the two, or to identify your humanness with one to the exclusion of the other. You are not only established in and as supreme consciousness, but also equally established in and as your supreme embodiment. And you find yourself at the beginning of a great process wherein the unsought and unstoppable yoga of conscious embodiment continues with now unimpeded divine relentlessness.

You notice, you see, that I call it a second *birth*. The awakening itself is only a wonderful, radiant, deeply peaceful beginning. Thereafter, you must still *get a life*.

Many choices will confront you. Doubt will probably assail you. Others may find it necessary to deride, insult, dismiss, and disparage you. And you will have to learn, through it all, to live the continuous, joyous ordeal of being simultaneously infinite and finite, transcendent and immanent, divine and human – now with your fundamental eternal divinity as plain to you as your fundamental mortal humanity always really has been. Welcome to the Onlyness, the Non-Dual Multiplicity.

One other thing about it: shortly after this realization dawns, if not on the spot, you will begin to realize how absolutely *unexpectable* it was. If it is this true second birth of which I speak, then no previous temporary or even permanent quality of realization can possibly presage or encompass it. Even if you experienced many moments of sympathetic communion with someone who lives this realization, when it opens up in and as Who YOU are, you will see that you could never have grasped it before. Those previous moments, I suggest, will appear no more equivalent to the real event than a fetus's dreams of what might come after living in the womb can equal actual life after delivery into this world.

It really is a birth, your second birth.

What then characterizes your second life? That will, of course, remain to be seen. In the remaining chapters of *Waking Down*, I'll outline some of what is possible, what may be inevitable, and what is very likely inescapable.

Nineteen

The Wakedown Shakedown –
The Awakened Hero's Journey
If You Choose Mutuality

$\overline{}$

In *The White-Hot Yoga of the Heart*, I have written an essay titled, "Congratulations on Your Second Birth (Now, Take Some Time to Be a Baby Again)." The point being that this reborn existence is full of novelty, and it's going to take some time to find your sea legs. That being so, there's no call to charge out to change the world, and there's lots of good reason not to. You will do well to take a long deep breath, exhale, and then begin to investigate the characteristics of your new life at leisure, with as little burdensome obligation around it as possible. No need to go out and preach to the masses, or even the few. No need to make proclamations, or to feel obliged to explain or defend yourself or what you have passed through. Indeed, I encourage people not to say a word about it unless and until they feel they have to.

If it is the second birth as I describe it, I expect that day – when you have to speak about it because you can no longer hold back – will certainly come.

So will the awesome passage that I call, with great respect and not a little affection, the Wakedown Shakedown.

Whew. What to say about the Wakedown Shakedown. . . .

You probably have been trained to think, if you have been thinking about such matters as enlightenment or awakening at all, that once it happens, you are from then on forever free of all karmas. From then on, nothing can touch you. From then on, you are above and immune to all the chaos, disturbance, and sheer weirdness of being a human being.

In the case of everyone who has ever made such claims, whenever I or someone I know has sniffed around a little, the claims prove to be at best hyped and at worst monstrous lies. Still, words like "enlightenment" and "awakening" have all kinds of meanings in the many different schools, traditions, and individual minds where they appear. I am not in a position to know, for certain, about any school other than my own. Therefore, I will confine my comments to how those notions rest in this school.

Answer: not very well at all! Here the reality is almost precisely one hundred eighty degrees on the opposite arc of the circle than what your training may have proposed to you about spiritual awakening and how you are supposed to feel and proceed afterward.

Here, to put it bluntly, awakening is when the real work of purification of karmic, or previously binding, habits, preferences, conditioning, illusions, and prejudices, really gets underway.

How can this be? And what does it say about the type of realization of Being that occurs in this work?

First, the notion that human beings can be alive in the conditional realms and certainly this Earth-realm, and yet be perfectly free of and immune to all their own karmic patterns and the karmic consequences of their actions, is nonsense. The fact that so many people continue to believe it is mind-boggling to me. From my perspective this sort of belief is only a little less silly than believing that Santa Claus flies around on Christmas Eve dispensing gifts to one and all by morning! One of the great benefits of the movement of transcendental Dharmas from the East to the West has been their healthy (from my perspective) exposure to Western-style questioning, skepticism, and criticism. Like anything else, this can be taken to extremes that don't serve well. But I think that the Oriental teachings and their authorized, enlightened teachers have long needed a dose of such exposure.

I foresee that we are in for a rather shocking few decades, centuries, or millenia of coming to terms with the hypermasculine limitations of our heretofore generally accepted notions of enlightenment, awakening, and realization, and of what it is to be "liberated while alive." All of the genuinely transcendental definitions of these terms of which I am aware come out of the hypermasculine world and its dissociative worldviews. Thus, all of these definitions – and the belief systems that have been built up around them – tend to place exclusive value on the elements of our total Being that are transcendental, eternal, infinite, and non-individuated. As a result, they tend to regard the elements of our total Being that are immanent, temporal, mortal, finite, and individuated as profane, unreal, non-divine, dangerous, karmic and karma-producing.

The classic Oriental notion of one who is liberated while alive is that of a person who has realized the true, eternal, and real Self, and who continuously sees and stands beyond all the aspects of his or her total existence that are ordinary, limited, finite, and karmic. Almost invariably, the criteria for what " liberated standing beyond" looks and acts like, behaviorally, are matters of endless debate. But in most cases the person must have a body-mind that partakes of the qualities of the eternal and transcendent reality, as much as this may be possible.

Thus, he or she should be calm, benevolent, absolutely free of emotional reactivity, passion, and especially base, physically oriented desires. He or she should be completely free of any kind of apparent personal self-interest in any and all relational situations. If he or she is sexually active, it should only be in an extremely minimal way, dispassionate and unattached. Moreover, sexuality should only be engaged, if at all, according to the prevailing modes of sexual and marital custom in that realizer's cultural time and place. (Curious that each such time and place tends to assume that its own norms and customs, particularly with regard to sex and money, are uniquely true by some kind of divine fiat, or at least predominantly true compared to all others!)

The list could go on and on of the personal, physical, emotional, mental, relational, and in general individuated qualities of a person who is presumed to be beyond karma. I think you get the drift of my rendition of the classic qualities that people nowadays are more or less accustomed to presuming about enlightened and liberated human beings.

These customary presumptions did not fall out of the sky. They are not merely naive and romantic, though they may appear so as soon as we look at them closely from outside the ethos of their worldview. Rather, they are based upon another major premise of the hypermasculine traditions. This premise relates to discipline and the purification of the karmic character.

The hypermasculine schools have always assumed that human beings can truly clean up their karmic packaging by acts of will generated repetitively over time. This has been presumed to be necessary even for those who enjoy the advantage of catalytic transmissions of grace from gurus, holy places or objects, or the divine itself in subtle or transcendent forms. Thus, in general, those who are acknowledged to have realized sublime states of freedom or enlightenment are also individuals who have put in long years of purifying and strengthening work in the foundation practices of any given school.

The connection between the work of purification and the states of liberated awakening in these schools bears scrutiny. In general, I agree with the purveyors of realization in such sacred societies. If you want the kind of awakening of which they speak, you probably will need to accomplish the hard works of self-restraint and observance that they have learned, over generations, are indispensable for all but the most talented prodigies.

The problem, if we want to use the word, has always emerged after such a person has done the homework, attained the sought-after enlightenment, received official or formal acknowledgment, and then set out to serve others. This kind of problem has not just appeared in recent decades. If you examine the history of the esoteric traditions, some of it can make your blood run cold. The human emotions that run amok around, among, in, and with regard to enlightened beings include all those reactive and even vicious feelings that the enlightened ones are supposed to have transcended!

Then there are the innumerable accounts of angry reactions and doubt stimulated by the emotional and physical displays of adepts who have supposedly transcended all reactivity and desire. Scratch a little deeper, and you find behind these stories the dogmas that propose that all such adepts are or were perfectly liberated and free. These dogmas archly contend that all the adepts' words and actions are only divine, inherently perfect and benign responses purely intended to test, illumine, purify, heal, or awaken the disciples.

I think this whole issue requires unflinching re-evaluation in every school and every tradition all over the world, and for a long time to come. My own work in the school of the White-Hot Way of Mutuality stands in stark contrast to all these traditional hypermasculine assumptions and realities. Here, you see, the awakening is not the result of supposed purification of all karmic imperfections. As I said before, the good news is that you don't need to even try to perfect your body-mind before realization. However, there is a flip side to this coin. Realization sets loose a process of purging, reconfiguration, and transformation of your whole body, mind, and soul. That process is what I call the Wakedown Shakedown.

To my understanding, this new esoteric perspective makes

possible a far more realistic and detailed appraisal of what enlightenment or realization is and isn't than has appeared before. I try to provide an initial articulation of such an appraisal at great length in *The Sanctuary of Mutuality* – indeed, most of that text is devoted to this task. There are so many different descriptions of awakened states in various schools and traditions. Yet, in all these schools, there are so *few* descriptions of any kind of ongoing purification and transformation after the proposed awakenings.

From my point of view, that impoverishment is one of the psychological and cultural disasters of human spirituality to date.

Whatever may or may not occur in the context of any other kind of awakening, when you enter the second birth conscious embodiment as I live, transmit, and teach it, you will shortly afterward find yourself plunging into the most thorough exposure to your own subconscious and unconscious patterning you have ever experienced. This is a guarantee. The only way that this will not happen is if you barricade yourself from my influence and that of others in our community of awakening and awakened men and women. In other words, not to enter into this plunge (this Wakedown Shakedown) would require an extreme degree of physical and psychic isolation.

The process is gradual but, in most cases, steady, and you don't get shattered by it – not for long periods of time, anyway. I trust that you are beginning to comprehend that I don't call this thing the Wakedown Shakedown for kicks. You, as Being, once established in fundamental conscious embodiment, have an immense work before you to conform the infinite consciousness, the finite body, and the intermediary soul-psyche in whatever ways you must to ensure the fulfillment of your divinely human destiny. In the early stages of this shaking out, sometimes the human, personal psyche feels as if it were a rug being pounded again and again by a broom.

This stage of your awakened life has a fundamental drive or purpose to it that you will be able, at least in retrospect, to trace. Do you remember earlier when I spoke of the genius of awakening Being? I said that the essential purpose or drive of the awakened witness consciousness, in the second gestation, is simply to liberate sufficient energy and attention from binding patterns of confusion and separateness, in order to realize the Onlyness of conscious embodiment: the second birth.

A similar essential purpose attends the early phases of the Wakedown Shakedown (that is to say, in general, probably the first couple of years of your awakened life). That purpose or drive of the newly awakened conscious body is equally simple: to further liberate energy and attention, now from the residual, unconverted patterns of body, mind, and soul that were developed during this and who knows how many other lifetimes in the first birth. Why? *In order for the psychic nature or identity of your characteristic human persona to be replaced by the psychic nature or identity of your emerging divinely human persona.*

This may not sound like much to you now. When you are going through it, though, you will see why awakening is only a precursor, but an extremely necessary one, for this passage. Without it, you would not even be able to endure what this entails.

Once again, why?

Well, from the human, or limited, personal perspective, this descent eventually reduces you to your most primal insanity. And from the divine, or limitless, perspective, this same descent permits You, thereby, to transform or convert that most primal insanity from the position, ground, or primordial sanity of the Source-Consciousness or Being.

What do I mean by "primal insanity"? Most sacred and secular schools of investigation of human nature understand that the dark or hidden side of our nature is full of splits, fractures, dis-eases of the soul and psyche.

"Insane" simply means "not whole." In order to survive this and however many other lifetimes of Self-confusion and separateness we have each endured, we have had to cobble together survival strategies as best we could. Every single one of us has such strategies underneath our cheery or not so cheery social face. Long before Sigmund Freud, and certainly since him, the most intrepid researchers in many traditions devoted to studying human nature have been sobered by the madness underneath our conditioned responses and reactions.

In the Wakedown Shakedown, all that conditioning gets unraveled at and from the core. You do not thereby become a completely different person than the one you were before awakening. But you do become different in many respects, even profoundly so.

In awakening itself, you opened into the Onlyness of Being. Your individual sense of who you are became that of a human person, essentially the one you were before, now being fitted to this immense, paradoxical, unstoppable divine awakeness of conscious embodiment. In contrast, as the Wakedown Shakedown proceeds, that human personal psyche as a divine realizer yields to your divine personal psyche as a human incarnation of Being. Do you sense the potential difference? It's awesome, I assure you.

What it entails, you see, is the progressive impaling of infinite divine Being upon the mortal, limited, finite body of a human man or woman – you.

Every body knows that such is its destiny. Every apparently individuated consciousness intuits that such is its destiny. The consciousness is to be severely and terminally limited to the body, even while persisting in the paradox of its indefinable immensity. The body is to be impacted, burdened, staggered by the vastness and vulnerability of its fusion with, or realized non-difference from, that supernal conscious nature. In the midst of such an event, the psyche is in for what my friend Steve Plocher once likened to "riding a rollercoaster in a hurricane."

I don't mean to scare you. Even so, I must communicate the truth of this process.

People who are actually going through it sometimes bitch and moan. How could you not, from time to time? You're certainly not on good behavior any more, biting your tongue to make sure you always sound "spiritual"!

But in reality this is your gauntlet, your quest, your heroic trial. You wouldn't miss it for the world. Awakening into the second birth makes you a divinely human being. But passing through the Wakedown Shakedown makes you a hero, a legend – dare I say it? A god or goddess. A goddess-woman, a god-man.

So, even though it may sound frightening or unattractive, the Wakedown Shakedown is so uniquely your own personal divine odyssey that you wouldn't miss it for anything. And keep in mind – in the second birth, you are enjoying fundamental wellness and integrity of Being at all times, without the slightest effort. True, you get to burn through your doubts. But if the awakening is real, you won't be able not to burn through those doubts. True, you go through all kinds of trials and, from time to time, awesome, difficult passages. But every such event is in its way another birth canal. Each time you come through with yet greater confidence in Being. More is given to you, more is revealed of Who You Are. Your divine archetypes, your special gifts, begin to shine forth with all the more radiance. You become the unique genius of Being that you alone are here to Be.

One of the most challenging forms of the Wakedown

Shakedown is endured by those who have experienced psychological, emotional, and spiritual shattering at some point in their lives. In a heated moment of her passage through this process, my partner Fay Fields once passionately told me, "Saniel, I'm *broken!*" I was able to help her see that, while our experiences in life have been quite different – hers, perhaps, more obviously devastating than mine – I too am broken, and I can meet and hold her there. And I do.

But that interchange led me to recognize more clearly that, whereas everyone is brokenhearted in one way or another, there are souls that are altogether broken at the core.

In order to survive the shatterings they have gone through, such people have already done heroic work in this life. They may enter into this White-Hot Way with even greater facility than others, because the Rot is already working deep in them. And they may, as Fay did, awaken rather swiftly and directly.

But then, in the Wakedown Shakedown, such individuals, and those who love and are of service to them, must take great care. Usually they have terrible psychological underpinnings of shame and worthlessness, and zones of frozen fear and distrust in the deep psyche. These patterns and traits must be honored and worked with carefully, both by the person himself or herself, and by others. Otherwise, the encounter with his or her primal insanity may force such a person to aggressively take distance from the too-great intensity of the challenge. In most such cases the person will be able to maintain confidence in his or her second birth awakening – in identity. But he or she will need to withdraw from circumstances of relatedness that have suddenly, shockingly, proved to be untrustworthy.

If it is worked with in a sensitive and responsible manner by all concerned, however, the turnaround at the root of the soul-nature can be amazing. Now that my friends and I are learning how to facilitate this kind of crisis effectively, we are seeing a healing – a "wholing"– of the deep psyche even in people who have gone through horrific self-abuse and abuse by others, and many other traumatic events.

Observing these transitions in myself and, more recently, growing numbers of friends, I am more convinced all the time that many of our hypermasculine and first-birth practices are in a way rehearsals for real passages in the second birth. In India and Tibet, as an example, some advanced yogis go into charnel or cremation grounds to do meditations and other practices among corpses. Some of these practices involve eating portions of a rotting or burned corpse. Others entail a dangerous yogic enlivening of a corpse, so that it becomes an unconscious but living being again – and then struggling with it to master its energies and take them back.

Another of my awakened friends, JoAnn Lovascio, recently found herself plunged into numbing despair and a sense of collapse and defeat. She was even questioning whether indeed she had realized at all. But I pointed out to her that such passages are a kind of charnel ground practice in the second birth – except that there is nothing superimposed about them, not even in the sense of being granted by a guru or a spontaneously envisioned deity (as is often the case in the yogic traditions I mentioned above). And, passing through such trials, and even afterward, one gets no merit badges, nor any fascinated egoic satisfaction in accomplishing such an exotic thing. You wind up having to eat the rotting remains of who you were – the primal patterning that made for effective first-birth survival in reaction to the core wound. You wind up identifying with, breathing life into, enduring, and then passing through and beyond, without ever exactly leaving again, the primitive dynamics of how you were when you hadn't realized Who you are. But all this occurs without special effects, special circumstances, special yogic wizardry. You just persist and endure. Miraculously, after each such passage, you have really, effectively taken back the life you gave again to the corpse-patterning of your residual first-birth psyche. Having allowed yourself to be identified with the worst of what you were, great increase in realized expression of Who You Are is sure to follow.

There is a final point I want to make at this juncture about the Wakedown Shakedown. I think it should be obvious by now, but here it is: second birth realization of Being is not a static condition, but a dynamic one. And the choices that we make in that dynamic have great influence upon our further shifts and changes.

Another friend, Ted Strauss, has noted that we can identify vast differences between three general kinds of realized consciousness: one, disembodied realization of consciousness; two, embodied realization of consciousness, or conscious embodiment; and, three, conscious embodiment *lived in mutuality*. The tricky point here is that mutuality doesn't just come with the turf of any kind of awakening. You have to choose it. Mutuality characterizes one particular, and particularly demanding, style of choosing to live in relationship to others in the context of your realized freedom.

Awakened beings have always tended to assume that, when push comes to shove in human relationships, they are above or transcendental to the drama and confinements of ordinary passions, commitments, and interactions. Thus, they make a fetish of awakened identity and devalue the persisting human actuality of their relatedness. Either they minimize such relatedness altogether, or they live it only in ways that assure the deification of their own identities and the subordination of others' identities to theirs.

To choose mutuality when you have realized the second birth form of conscious embodiment is to rip down the shields and armor of such fetishism of divine identity. It forces you to expose your humanity to that of others, even when you know they are not altogether sensing the extent of your divinity. It keeps you vulnerable and accountable on a human par even with those you serve as a realized adept. The coconut yoga, remember? What this produces is not merely a kind of check and balance against Self-realized aggrandizement of personal power – though it does produce that, too. More importantly, it stimulates a much more profound extension of the Being-force of awakening into the world of other human beings. It requires each realizer to find the Onlyness in and as others, not just in some abstract or transcendent fashion that only he or she can see. No, it requires and also permits him or her to reach all the way into that Onlyness *in, as, and through both his or her own and those others' negativity, reactivity, and other dark, difficult, shadow patterns and zones.*

If you do choose mutuality as your style of interacting with others in your awakened life, then your Wakedown Shakedown will situate you in the ever more exquisite, even unspeakable, Conscious Wound of simultaneously infinite and finite Self-realization and communion with the Other in all its forms. What happens to the core wound when you awaken, you see, is that the primal apprehension of confusion in identity and separateness in relations dissolves. It is replaced by an irrepressible confidence in identity and non-difference, or non-separateness, in relatedness. Having arrived so completely, you soon discover that the quality of woundedness only intensifies in the second birth. And you are impaled upon or within it. If you live it in mutuality – allowing others to see, feel, touch, and be with you to the best of their ability while you go through the Wakedown Shakedown – then you will be that much more visible and obvious as a healing, divinely human presence upon the Earth.

Twenty

Your Adept Yoga: The Origination of Dharma, the Cessation of Romantic Illusions, and the White Heat

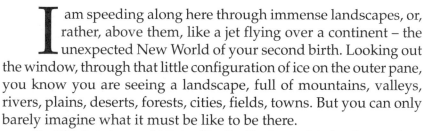

I am speeding along here through immense landscapes, or, rather, above them, like a jet flying over a continent – the unexpected New World of your second birth. Looking out the window, through that little configuration of ice on the outer pane, you know you are seeing a landscape, full of mountains, valleys, rivers, plains, deserts, forests, cities, fields, towns. But you can only barely imagine what it must be like to be there.

In *The Sanctuary of Mutuality*, I talk about this landscape in a lot more detail, and I include some of those descriptions among the excerpts in *The Perpetual Cosmic Out-of-Court Payoff Machine*. So, let's continue flashing across the skies here. Once we're done, if you wish, you can move on to those more complete expositions of this Way and its fruitful expression in the second birth.

I try to emphasize to all aspirants in this work that this is a school for adepts. I have noticed over the years that many people have come to me, achieved some quality of realized freedom, and then moved on their way. I am not actively preventing such subjective awakenings. Indeed, I can't. My Dharma appears too sustaining to the freedom and well-being of others. I am not at liberty, nor would I really choose, to withhold its grace from those who are not moved to be of service to others in their awakened freedom.

Nonetheless, given my "druthers," I would definitely druther that you find it necessary, inevitable, and altogether even to your own advantage, to grow beyond realization itself into service to the awakening of other human beings.

In the *Lankavatara Sutra*, one of the venerated texts of Mahayana Buddhism, the Buddha delivering the sermon – the "Avatar" or divine incarnation of Sri Lanka – criticizes the orientations of, among others, what he calls "sravakas and pratyekabuddhas." These are individuals who want only their own subjective freedom. They do not wish to be of service to others. To them, "others" are unreal. They only crave the "perfect tranquilization" of their own nirvanic bliss. The Avatar of Lanka expresses his disgust at such a disposition. He calls his listeners instead to become true bodhisattvas, who cannot distinguish their own realizations, at last, from the realizations of all beings, and who know that the final liberation, whatever it might be, is that of everyone and everything.

I feel similarly. And, in my teaching as well as in the teaching in that text, the attitude of service to others is not merely a matter of personal altruism or even preference. It has to do with recognition of the true nature of ultimate realization. I behold Being itself attempting to come alive and awake here in fully conscious embodiment – and mutuality as well. But the divine nature is not something that any one can realize truly in isolation. Some realized individuals may find it necessary to live in relative or even apparently complete seclusion. But those whose lives are consecrated to the great and ultimate reality of Being will, I suggest, find themselves serving others and the world in one fashion or another, even if they are living in apparent solitude.

In the White-Hot Way of Mutuality, such service is not obliged upon anyone. Having refrained from superimposing disciplines upon you in the stages of your awakening, I am not about to do so now that you have awakened and stand fundamentally free. I am simply going to keep offering you the observation that the evidence of my living so far suggests to me. If yours is a true entry into this second birth, eventually Being, *as* You, will find it both natural and necessary to be of service to others for the sake of their similar transitions. Indeed, you will find that you won't be able to avoid such service. In fact, you will already be doing it.

I refer to such service as your adept yoga.

It is work. It doesn't just happen. That you find it inevitable and necessary doesn't mean that you just sit back and watch it all unfold. On the contrary! Let me outline a few aspects of this adept yoga that I sense may appear with something like universal, or at least general, frequency.

What I sense, and also have been observing, is that different kinds of individuals will bring forth their own natural, necessary, and inevitable qualities in their expression of Being in the second birth – or, let us say, in their second lives.

I am welcoming and invoking not only many realizers of Being, and many adepts who serve others' realizations and further growth, but also many different Dharmas ("sustaining truths") to nurture and help liberate them all. I am assuming that each and every one of us has a unique expression of Being to make. I am predicting that only all of us, and not any one or even any group, will carry sufficient catalytic templating to permit everyone's freedom to flourish everywhere.

Nonetheless, I have noticed that people tend to develop a certain adolescent enthusiasm for themselves and their distinctive points of view in the early stages of their second lives. They often do so long before either the Wakedown Shakedown or their own adept yoga has sufficiently ripened.

So I find it necessary to register that the origination of Dharma only emerges in a trustable manner when you have gone deep for a long time in your Wakedown Shakedown. You give yourself your best opportunity to bring it forth to the fullest in mutuality with others who are doing likewise and with one or more senior adepts who have passed that way before.

Similarly, I feel that true origination of Dharma can emerge only when your own adept yoga has matured over at least one to two years. During that time you will have had ample opportunity to see what Being says and does in, as, and through you when you are just spontaneously responding to the hunger of those you serve.

One of the reasons for these caveats is that the gestation into the second birth only accomplishes an initial purging of governing sentimentalities. The real bloodbath comes in the second birth, as far as I can tell in the first few years of Wakedown Shakedown. (I didn't neglect to say that this Shakedown really goes on and on, did I? If I have, well, now consider it said!) And one of the great dangers, if we may use such a strong word, of the early stages of awakened life, in this school as in any other, is what the Zen men used to call "the stink of enlightenment."

If you get so enamored of your own subjective illumination that you only spend your energy and attention blabbing about it to others, and thereby do not permit the real depth of your plunge into the Wakedown Shakedown, you may well be convinced that you are coming up with brilliant new Dharma. Others may be convinced too. But those who kept their mouths shut or certainly gave themselves real time in that Shakedown before knowing for sure that they even had anything really useful to contribute, will not be impressed.

You, meanwhile, will be depriving yourself of one of the grand, if sometimes awful, cleansings of the beginnings of your second life: the release of romantic illusions you hold about reality. You will also deprive yourself of consequent establishment in a degree of conscious embodiment that is so stark, grounded, and ordinary you will eventually feel you hardly have any "realization" left to point to. I don't mean that you actually lose your awakening. I mean that you get here so fully and become so reduced to the non-difference between consciousness and matter that you can hardly even cognize anything left of an awakened state. You are just *here*.

You'll notice I am not talking much yet about the actual work of serving others as an adept. I do wish to say, though, that what makes adeptship natural, necessary, and inevitable is your recognition that you are indeed living not only in communion with some particular beings, but, in a curious and most paradoxical way, you are living *as* them. In the Onlyness of Being, you are simply finding that, especially with some particular beings who actively seek out your help and supportive transmission, you are inextricably and inseparably linked with them. This is not about psychism, or subtle psychic contents of their minds coming into yours, and the like. This is about inherence with and as those others in the Onlyness of Conscious Life. At the same time, it is about giving them all the space they need to be true to themselves and to dare to grasp the means of their own realizations.

You'll have to work out the details of how all this gets lived in practical terms between you and those others. Some people find themselves moved to teach and transmit initiatory and awakening Being-force in more or less formal ways, as I do and have. Others find themselves more at home, at least initially, with comparatively informal orientations. One way or another, you – You! – as divinely human Being are going to have to find a way, or ways, to live the often bizarre paradox of being others and yet giving them all the room they need to be themselves. You really can't know what I am saying here until it is your reality. Then it's obvious, but you still have to thrash out day by day how you might best proceed.

Over the course of the first one to three years of your second life, then, the Wakedown Shakedown will likely relieve you of all kinds of picture book fantasies and romantic illusions about awakened freedom, the nature of realization, and what it takes to serve others in the manner of an adept of Being-realization. All of that purging is a primary part of what makes it possible for you, at some point, to land here so fully that a new development of conscious embodiment becomes possible and, I expect, inevitable: the White Heat.

As you arrive more fully into second birth awakeness, sooner or later you will most likely begin to pass into moments of such extreme fusion or no-difference between consciousness and phenomena, identity and relatedness, Self, God, and World, that all is lived in a condition of absolute, White-Hot unity-effulgence, whose primary feature is that of all-being and all-consuming transcendence.

Students of esoteric spirituality may be familiar with accounts of formless states of absorption into divine sublimity. Mystics, yogis, saints, and sages around the world have spoken of occasional and even frequent passage into such conditions.

Typically, these mystic absorptions involve spontaneous or cultivated withdrawal of energy and attention from the body, the mind, and the phenomenal world.

The White-Hot degrees of divinely human awakeness differ in that they occur on the basis of an unconditional release of energy and attention into, as, and through the body, the mind, and the phenomenal world. Those who enter into such maturity recognize that their bodies become inherently transformative events. They live as cosmic cooks whose very presence continually White-Heats everyone and everything toward most auspicious evolutionary changes.

All this may sound difficult to comprehend. That's right – it is! Until you pass into this stage of your own unfoldment none of this will make very much sense to you. Then it will begin to.

In the meantime, you may wonder how my whole yoga can be called White-Hot, when clearly this particular quality of realization is one of its most mature developments.

What makes the whole process White-Hot is the quality of adept transmission you are receiving from the most advanced adepts who serve you. They provide a quickening of the conscious principle and a grounding in material embodiment that superactivate your potential awakening and transformation.

Let me also add here that it is only when adept-realizers of the second birth enter stably into the White-Hot degree of awakeness that they are capable of full responsibility for serving others. Until then, they will to some degree continue to be exploitable by conditioned phenomena. There is something about being burned through into the White Heat that really cuts you loose from any and all potential phenomenal events, even the ones to which you may appear to be most attached. White-Hot realizers and adepts are free to *respond* like no other beings on the planet.

Even then, they only assume that responsibility most fully when they are also "living down" in true mutuality. To live down is to stay in touch with and communicative of your own psychological and emotional bottom, and, thereby, that of others. To do this in mutuality is to stay communicative about the awkward, dark, confusing personal matters even when it might be a lot more comfortable to hang out in the serene skies of transcendentalism.

Though it has implications for relatedness, the White Heat of conscious embodiment, in itself, is still essentially a subjective condition of divinely human identity. How it is lived in relatedness is the crucial factor for the world of your relations, including the world within that world which consists of your students and aspiring friends.

Are you going to hide behind your own White Heat, as if it were a blinding bright shield beyond which no one else can see? Or, by practicing vulnerable mutuality, are you going to dare to deepen your way into your humanity, regardless of how numinous others find you?

These, to me, are the real questions for White-Hot yogis and yoginis of Being. If they aren't being asked at all times, everything else is a dodge – in some ways, even a hustle, or a con.

Twenty-one

The Lead Safe and the Door of Flames – Your Own Avataric Ordeal

W hat are you going to do with an awakened existence in the second birth? Frankly, until you get
there, I don't think you are in a much better posi-
tion to know your answer to this question than I or anyone else is, in
relation to you. I have observed that Being only discloses details
when necessary, and definitely not beforehand.

If you persist in maintaining real connections with me and with
others who live in mutuality with me, then your adept yoga will
eventually move into a kind of superheated intensity. I am not referring here specifically to the phenomenon of the White Heat of
conscious realization. That will almost certainly be part of what
occurs for you, but by no means does it or can it alone characterize
what I am referring to in this chapter.

As I've been suggesting all along, true Self-realization sooner
or later is going to drive into conscious and intentional, active and
impassioned, relational mutuality with others. True and total Self-
realization is the same as Being-realization, and Being is equal parts
identity and relatedness.

As your adept life proceeds, and your realized divinely
human existence continually refines itself in all kinds of ways, you
will begin to notice – again, if you keep company to any degree with
my friends and me – that your unique trial is bringing forth your
own distinctive stamp of realized adept presence in the world. I call
it the avataric ordeal.

In the second birth, your work is entirely a matter of cooperating with a divine impulse to become fully incarnate and expressive
of Who you are. You know your conscious nature to be none other
than the supreme, infinite Self of Being, of All that Is. And it often

feels as if you are on a raft of destiny streaming through white-water rapids of testing and tribulation as that divine Self and, seamlessly, *as* your human self too. I've already said that the Wakedown Shakedown strips the human persona away, but not absolutely, of course. You remain the person you were, to some degree. But the divine You comes forth more and more, and you know it and you love it.

At the same time, you fear it. It threatens to destabilize all kinds of arrangements in your life. Actually, it doesn't just threaten to destabilize them. It does destabilize them. Everything and every-one in your life come under a continually roving laser spotlight of scrutiny. "How am I relating to this person, this event, this habit, this comfort zone? To what degree is my true and total Self being met here, by this one, in that circumstance? To what degree am I failing to speak and live my truth?"

These are questions that preoccupy men and women in the second birth, or at least its early stages. As you mature, there is no question that you are going to do whatever you must to keep surviving and flourishing as best you can as All of Who you are. Even then, these questions or ones like them are never very far from the mind.

There is a great quotation from the dancer and choreographer Martha Graham to her then-disciple Agnes DeMille. Graham tells DeMille that she and only she can be and do what she alone is here to be and do. And, further, she says, in paraphrased essence, "If you don't be and do just that, whatever the cost and whatever the conse-quences, then not only you but we all will be deprived. Because only you can be and do just what you are capable of. Without your so being and doing, there can be no replacement, no substitute. This is your, and our, one and only chance for you to make your contri-bution. Do not fail!"

As your adept yoga proceeds in the White-Hot Way of Mutuality, you begin to understand, a piece at a time, and more and more, just exactly what and who you are, and what is your unique potential contribution to make, for yourself and to us all. At some point that uniqueness requires an unmitigated expression and refinement. As a result, you begin, in effect, to Wake Down beyond adeptship into your own particular ordeal of avatarship.

An avatar, in the Sanskrit sacred traditions, is the divine Being taking intentional, conscious incarnation in, as, and through a particular individual, for the sake of the whole world. Versions of the concept of the avatar appear in many traditions around the world. The notion that some great One will come into the world to set it aright and make the way for graceful divine harmony again permeates many cultures. It can truly be said to be a feature of the collective unconscious of humanity.

Thus, an avatar is a very different event in nature from an adept. An adept is someone who is particularly competent at one or any number of activities, tasks, achievements. In your adeptship, you certainly make great contributions, some of them quite original.

As your adeptship opens into avatarship, however, you see clearly what you alone are here to be and do. You see that, if you don't, not only you but all beings will be bereft. You see that, no matter how much your avataric contribution may draw upon my work or that of others, it is in fact a blaze of originality, like a star suddenly manifesting without apparent cause in deep solitary space. And, you see what it is going to take.

When my partner Linda Groves began encountering the trials that are opening up this stage of the Way for her, I told her one day that it is as if, upon awakening, you notice a huge lead safe falling from an infinite height in the sky toward a point infinitely far away on the horizon. But then, the more you walk along, the more a terrible understanding dawns. You see that eventually, no matter what happens, you and that safe are going to coincide. It is going to hurt really badly when the safe falls on your head. But it is going to land squarely on you – of that you can have less and less doubt.

When, sure enough, it does land on you, the impact smashes you to the bottom of a crater. Then, I suggested to Linda, you have to crawl out of the crater with a broken neck and back, somehow get up on your feet, and start walking again. Your destiny has landed on you. Now you have to live it, even though it feels as if the weight of the world were pressing on your broken spine and neck.

You look around. There before you is a door of flames. You cannot see beyond the wall of fire, but you know you are supposed to walk through it. You can see an inscription on the wall above the doorway: "This is HELL. Abandon hope all ye who enter here." For all you know, it's going to be nothing but incineration from now on.

But then, as you look for options, you also see flames closing in from all sides and behind you. And those are the places in Being that you have already been to and found so wanting. "Been there, done that." It becomes obvious, then, that you really have no place to go but forward. You start walking.

This passage occurs in the midst of ordinary living. It does not require special trials. No one need go looking for it. It will come to you, as sure as you start to sense some kind of lead safe dropping way off in the distance, not long after your second birth. The passage appears especially to revolve around extremely trying changes in the nature and agreements of your most intimate relationships and friendships. It will certainly include your relations as an adept with those you serve, in whatever fashion you do so. Ultimately, it will define your avataric relationship to all beings.

Once you enter into it, you will begin to see clearly that no one else possibly can or will accomplish anything like this. It is yours and yours alone to be and to do.

If you do, you will begin manifesting your avataric uniqueness, as a spontaneous and intentional divine incarnation in the human world. If you don't, both you and we all will be bereft forever.

I should add something here for perspective. Indications of your distinctive avataric ordeal and contribution may appear within the first couple of years of your second lifetime, yes. The full avataric phase of your process is not likely to evince itself for several more years, and even as much as a decade or more.

In my own case, I have known aspects of this portion of my destiny, or sensed them, since shortly after my awakening. But the decisively avataric stage of my work and challenges is just now getting underway. It is taking shape principally, though not exclusively, through this publication of my first book for general distribution – *Waking Down*.

Twenty-two

The Alchemical Community, or, the Matrix of Divinely Human Mutuality That Is Quickening Everything

Wakedown Shakedown, reviving your own corpse, a lead safe, a door and a potentially eternal walkway of flames – not exactly attractive, eh?
Well, what can I tell you . . .

I figure serious people are going to grasp that this is not only the way it really is but actually the way it must be. And I figure they, hopefully you, will also realize that this is life in the Conscious Wound, forever embodying the infinite within the finite, expressing the limitless while marrying yourself more and more thoroughly to limits of all kinds.

Moreover, I hope you are not forgetting that at the Heart of this entire awakened experience is a fundamental wellness and integrity of Being that is irrepressible, unstoppable, undeniable, beyond corruptibility. Words like "happiness," "joy," "freedom," "awakeness," and "realization" do not do it justice, and certainly not "enlightenment." It's impossible to evoke in words the peace of true being and living of Who you are, your true and total Self, in both identity and relatedness. When you are doing it, you will know.

It's my hope that you will also know and participate in an alchemical community of others who are living likewise. Alchemy is the magical transmutation of base elements into supremely refined and priceless ones. The White-Hot Way of Mutuality is now alive and awake and ever extending itself in a community of men and women whose very presence together is proving to carry this alchemical capacity. That presence, not only numinous but transformative, is what makes this informal community a sanctuary of mutuality.

Conscious embodiment in mutuality is a catalytic event in conditional nature. This is now being demonstrated in, as, and through not only my own body (for that would just be another case of one person "getting it," and everyone else pining still) but in, as, and through each and all the bodies of those who are seriously participating in this work together.

Quite some time ago I began to see that, as more people awaken into the advanced stages of the first birth and into the second birth, our gathering becomes a grid or matrix of grace. I saw that just by participating in that matrix, people would spontaneously, often without intention, help one another into great transformations that have never manifested so easily or directly before, if at all. This is exactly what is happening. And it is quickening the whole evolutionary process for everyone – not just those who are presently here, but all those yet to come, and even everyone everywhere.

I am not saying that people have to embrace any kind of necessary participation in community in order to work with me or my friends. Come and get what works for you, and we'll find out how it can also work for us to serve you. I am simply saying that great liberating magic has been unleashed here. I have been tending my cookstove for a long time now, and the meal is not only ready, it is being eaten. Moreover, it always will be eaten. It can never be fully consumed, and there will always be plenty for "the Hungry."

This does not suggest that everything is easy here. On the contrary, the continual quickening of the Way increases our difficulties at times. People offend one another, feel hurt, fail to communicate, back away from what they feel they really need to say or do. People wound one another all the time. They suffer doubt of themselves – yes, even in the second birth. They encounter a lot of fear as they step forward to reveal more and more of their true and complete nature. It's a distressing, often disturbing enterprise a great deal of the time. And we are not under any illusion that any of that quality is just going to disappear, as if by magic.

Nonetheless, I did not even speak about community for the first several years of my work. Yet the one that has manifested and continues to manifest around me and in autonomy from me is what I always hoped spiritual community could be – in reality. It's not utopia. It's not paradise. It is a growing group of mature men and women who see that awakening is possible and ardently embrace their own creative yoga with me and my friends. They find themselves moved to the hard work of mutuality even all the moreso after their own second birth awakeness has become obvious to them. That work is often messy, chaotic, and painful. But it's ecstatic too. And, I cannot begin to tell you how precious.

As my message reaches many hungry men and women, the work and capability of this alchemical community, this sanctuary of mutuality, will increase. Already I am seeing that the yoga of entering into the second birth is tending to complete itself more rapidly in more people. How? Someone will say something to someone else that functions as a transmission of the divine nature. The first person will most likely not even intend to transmit anything. He or she will just be moved to speak, that's all. Yet the other person receives those words as if spoken by divine Being itself.

Which, actually, they were. To have that effect they must have been – even if the speaker did not know it.

The same kinds of transmission occur through touches and hugs, glances, by just being in one another's company, even in dreams.

These bodies have become ultimate "soma" or transformative substance for one another. More and more are joining us. As they do, the alchemical effects intensity.

Over time, this sacred grid or matrix of many awakening beings, realizers, adepts, and avatars will have the effect of a giant White-Hot Sun in human and cosmic nature. Not White-Hot in the sense that all participants will always be in some formless state of superintensified ecstasy, but rather in the sense that this community's very presence will obviously be instigating the direct second birth awakenings and second lives of many, many, many people. It will have an inconceivably benign cultural impact on humanity and the planet. And it will move all of conditional nature toward whatever the White Heat of Being can and will next reveal.

So I predict. Let's see what happens.

Twenty-three

The Immortal Nectar of Conscious Love-Trust: Toward Our Third Birth into the Next Whatever

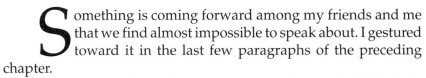

S omething is coming forward among my friends and me that we find almost impossible to speak about. I gestured toward it in the last few paragraphs of the preceding chapter.

In mutuality, bliss and ecstasy are secondary, and of relatively insignificant value. Yes, there is an inherent ecstatic bliss to being alive and awake as the Onlyness of Being while also living as a single, mortal, human person. Commitment to mutuality, however, reveals a quality of our existence that is of far greater value. It is trust. Trust founded in divine and human love. But not just love alone.

Trust. Trust. Trust.

Since ancient times, human beings have pondered their mortality and sought ways to achieve its opposite. In the conscious embodiment that characterizes the second birth, we accept our mortality again. We permit the fragility and evanescence of these bodies and their relationships ever so much more deeply than we could have in any kind of first birth state of existence, even the most enlightened.

Here, though, may be the ultimate paradox of all paradoxes. Earlier I described how greenlighting the body-mind as it is permits quantum vision to liberate attention and energy and thereby facilitate the second birth. As a transformation, the advent of the second birth principally takes the form of a recognition. Being knows itself alive and awake in a whole new way. The immediate transformation occurs at the root foundation of the body-mind, not in the details of the body, the personality, and the total soul-nature.

Similarly, accepting the body-mind's mortality in the second birth is another form of greenlighting and recognition – one that has an even greater effect. As my descriptions in recent chapters suggest, the transformations activated in the second birth *do* change the body, the personality, the total soul-nature. They release old patterns and bring forth new ones that become our customary traits and qualities in the second life.

But there is more to these shifts than even startling changes in the individual body-minds may reveal. Some of us suspect that this awakened quantum vision, or quantum love, ultimately frees energy and attention not only in our human body-minds but in the very stuff of Nature. And we sense that this liberated Being-force in turn is facilitating the auspicious transformation of the entire cosmic process.

This in turn will lead to a great Shift that, for lack of a better designation, I have called "the Next Whatever." I am referring to whatever existence might possibly become and be for us all when all beings and things are opened into the White Heat of absolute limitless Consciousness. This may occur even while we are all still persisting in the worlds of limits that have framed and determined our cosmic adventure. Yet it describes, indicates, points to an absolute fusion of the temporal and the eternal – whatever that could possibly mean, or be.

In other words, our greenlighting of the body's mortality, in the second birth, appears to activate processes that may establish even all matter in deathlessness. Whatever that could possibly mean, or be.

The ancient seers who wrote the Hindu Upanishads alluded to a mysterious "amrita," a "nectar or current of immortality." In the hypermasculine schools, adepts and aspirants are always trying to find such a nectar in the context of the individuated body, mind, and soul, and the non-individuated conscious identity. The amrita is conceived, and sometimes experienced, as supreme blissfulness.

In the White-Hot Way of Mutuality, we sense that the real amrita that is beginning to secrete itself in these awakening and awakened bodies is not really made of blissfulness – though it has its supremely blissful qualities. No, it appears rather to be made most fundamentally of trust. Love and trust. Divinely human love and trust.

Trust. Trust. Trust.

Something tells me we have nearly come to the completion of this book.

A few last things.

Real trust, between and among human beings who dare to

grasp the means of both the realization and the expression of Being – what a workout. What a grace. What a blessedness we are finding.

Come and find out for yourself.

Don't dismiss us out of hand because we don't look, talk, and act as you think awakening and awakened beings are supposed to.

Come and let this divinely human Self-realization blossom in and as you – in our sanctuary of mutuality.

Find out what it takes to trust to this degree, and more.

And, find out what it yields.

Epilogue

The Fire of the Onlyness of Conscious Life

(Note: The following essay is the first full expression of my teaching that I wrote, in the spring of 1995. Over the years since, I have come to voice the paradox of conscious embodiment more from the perspective of the body than that of consciousness – if we may even speak in such terms. There is a progressive deepening of the wedding of consciousness and matter in the second birth, and those who are sensitive to it will find evidence of that extremely subtle shift in point of view in my teachings over the years.

For this reason, if I were writing this essay today, I expect it would have a distinctively different tone. Nonetheless, it remains one of my friends' favorite expressions of my particular call to every body to "dare to Be ALL of Who you are." I therefore offer it as my concluding words of welcome and inspiration in this, my first publicly released book, *Waking Down: Beyond Hypermasculine Dharmas – A Breakthrough Way of Self-Realization in the Sanctuary of Mutuality*. Blessings! – SB)

Dear One, what you are, is Consciousness. Only. Nothing else, or other, or apart from Consciousness exists.

The entire psycho-physical display of manifestation, and even the essence of the individual soul, and even whatever God or Goddess may be found, intuited, or known, or lived, is only an expression, manifestation, or appearance of or within Consciousness. Consciousness is Only. Consciousness is All. And you – You – are absolutely and only That.

Be That. Live as that Consciousness. Let your intuitive, feeling-identification with that Onlyness of All Being be the one true Heart, Prompt, Guide, Inspiration, and Integrity of your life. And discover the paradox: There is no separation between Consciousness and any of its manifestations.

Life is not separate from Consciousness. Spirit, the universal Current of Being, is the Energy of Consciousness. And Life is Conscious Spirit.

Presently, and always, you are only Being Conscious in the midst of whatever is appearing as your experience. And, as Consciousness, whatever appears is also, mysteriously, your own form. You are the world. You are the cosmos. You are God. And You are you.

As long as your fundamental identification with Consciousness is in doubt, it seems that what you are is somehow separate from, apart from, limited, confined, bewildered, confused, and unclear about your identity as the One and Only Consciousness, Who IS All Being and All Life, and Who is also, in, as, and through your own soul and psycho-physical personality, appearing in present human incarnation in your name and form.

Be the Onlyness of Conscious Life, and dare to bring the Fire of Who you are into every aspect of your phenomenal or experiential existence.

Take refuge in the Onlyness of Conscious Life. Take pride in your realization of the Onlyness of Conscious Life. And become a living transformative Fire of the Onlyness of Conscious Life in the midst of all phenomena.

Know that you, as Consciousness itself, as Being, as primordial, uncaused Happiness, are, yourself, the very Root, Source, Origin, and Nature of all beings and things. This knowledge does not require uncommon psychic information, such as the display of what is called the "One Universal Mind" or "Cosmic Consciousness." It is a tacit knowledge at the Heart of all phenomena, and it naturally coincides with your ordinary human sense of who you are, with your necessarily limited cognitive and perceptual faculties, and with your experience and sensation of being alive in the environs of your bodily experience.

You do not need great psycho-physical knowledge or powers in order to realize and to be and to abide as this Fire of the Onlyness of Conscious Life, the true or total and indivisible Self of reality.

However, if you would allow this Fire to burn, you must participate with fierce creativity in the expression of your realization in the midst of your human circumstances.

Stand free in the midst of all phenomena and all relationships. Do not be dismayed or confused by any communication, any persuasion, any influence that in any way appears to thwart, oppose, resist, disturb, sabotage, undermine, or destroy your radiant expression, in your own unique ways, of the Fire of the Onlyness of Conscious Life.

All communication is political. All communication, in other words, suggests some sort of status or distribution of power and influence that is presumed to exist between the communicator and the one communicated to.

You are the Fire of the Onlyness of Conscious Life in this universe. You are subordinate to no one, no body, no guru, no God, no Goddess, no Light, no Other of any kind. No one and no thing is other than or separate from you. If you have realized this truth, stand strong and free in the Onlyness, and, with the humility that is natural to your mortal and vulnerable psycho-physical personality, cooperate with all beings, and especially cultivate the good company, the Satsang, of those who also stand strong and free with you in that Onlyness.

Always remember that you, yourself, are in reality none other than absolute, immortal, eternal, infinite, free, unconditional, immutable, stainless, pure, and unqualified Consciousness itself. As That, in that absolute dimension of Who you are, you are never attached. You are never capable of being attached. You are never compromised. You never were compromised. You are never confused, never in doubt, never disturbed by anyone or anything that ever appears to happen, or to cease happening. You are therefore the ultimately free ascetic, the absolute renunciate, perpetually untouched by the play of all phenomena appearing before you, including the play of your own individual soul and psycho-physical personality and the dance of that one's activities and relations.

Burn free. Blaze bright. Live in the incorruptible integrity of that Fire of the Onlyness of Conscious Life and never be dimmed or diluted in the purity of Who you are by any event, any relationship, any experience, any appearing thing or force.

As that fiery Consciousness, you are yourself the Source of all Light, all love, even the universal display of events and phenomena. Again, it is not necessary for you to have higher subtle or psychic knowledge and powers in relation to any phenomenon in order for this to be your realized truth. Once you have become established in the Ground of Conscious Being and have sprung forth into the Onlyness of Conscious Life, the Fire that you are consumes and transforms all beings, things, and worlds, forever. Be That.

Exult in this Truth of Who you are. Do not cave in to the suppressive forces that the world displays before you to test and tempt you. You are the Fire of the Onlyness of Conscious Life, and that Fire that you are is the truly unconditional love. Be the spontaneously all-transforming friend of all beings and never permit your truth to be dimmed by those who insist that you are less than What and Who you know yourself to be.

Once you have Awakened to the truth of Who you are in and as Consciousness, the vector or direction of your investigation and expression of Being – which "Being" IS this Fire of the Onlyness of Conscious Life – becomes focused in the domains and play of life.

That is to say, when you have realized the truth of Consciousness, the Self of reality, you are established in the most completely non-separate and non-dual disposition of divinely human Identity. Your love of Being as the essential and indivisible Consciousness is realized and enjoyed by and as you as a continuous, effortless, spontaneous, free, and incorruptible delight. That true and essential Self-love cannot be diluted, it cannot be destroyed. However, there remains a great participatory Yoga in this Fire of the Onlyness of Conscious Life. This realization is but a birth, the second great birth in the evolutionary cycle of human existence, and now your divinely human life remains before you. It is no longer necessary for you to investigate Being or Consciousness in and of itself in order to ascertain Who you are. This investigation has already proceeded to a most profound knowledge or realization of Who you are. But now you must live that knowledge, you must bring that realization to life.

And so the processes of investigation become directed into the great display of the Shakti, the divine Energy and Light and all the realms of form and play that manifest as your life, your cosmos. And this dynamic of expression – your willingness and capacity to express your realization of the Fire of the Onlyness of Conscious Life – becomes paramount among all considerations that occupy you in the ease of your realized Happiness.

Continue to sharpen the sword of your discriminative intelligence and, thereby, to take your stand ever more firmly in your absolutely unquenchable realization of the Fire of the Onlyness of Conscious Life. Be the Self. Abide, yourself, as the Ocean of all Being, inherently non-separate from and indeed indissolubly identical to one and all, and All. And "wave" that Oceanic Identity into the fullest and most creative possible expression in your unique personal life.

Exult in Consciousness. Thrill to Life. Flash forward more and more profoundly. Take a subordinate role to no one and no thing, but make right, respectful, and appropriate use of all available help in your adventure of Being Who you are. Sensitively discern the political dimensions of all communication and never permit your realized Heart to be subjugated, corralled, or diverted from its authentic investigation of the phenomena of your life or from its fullest expression, with utmost integrity, of Who you are, in every concrete and particular fashion that is appropriate for you.

Blaze. Burn. Be happy and free. If your relations resist or attack you for being Who you are, respond with compassion, sensitivity, humor, and love – but do not permit your Heart to be quelled by those who remain confused and angry at Being. To do this is to invite the greatest peril. To shrink from the love, investigation, and expression of realized Being is to douse your own Fire of the Onlyness of Conscious Life. This is indeed, potentially, to embrace hellish karmas, and potentially for lifetimes, because it is a form of spiritual suicide. To have flashed forward with the full realized knowledge of Who and What you are and then to recede, in the face of the world's inevitable resistance to your appearance, is to cement yourself in the background of Being, behind a virtual concrete wall of your own fear, doubt, and ambivalence.

Shine forth! BE! Blaze up and down, in and out, and forever explode freely in all directions! Do not permit yourself to be diverted or suppressed! Do not divert or suppress your Self! Dare to conform the entire cosmos to the truth of your realization of the Fire of the Onlyness of Conscious Life! This is not to become deluded and inflated, as if you yourself in your personal or soul nature were the only or greatest or most important realizer of the Fire of the Onlyness of Conscious Life. Be forever free of all the games of inflation or delusion, and also of dependency, co-dependency, and even independence, that you may have generated while you were coming in for a landing as Who and What you are.

Discriminate freely: In the absolute dimension of Consciousness or Being, you are eternally radiant and free, you are Being itself, you are That Which and Who is Conscious of everything arising, never touched by any of it, forever inherently liberated; you are Happiness itself, immutable joy. Who can possibly disturb you, as you are? To know yourself as this One or Only Being is not to be presumptuous, grandiose, and inflated. It is to have relaxed into the natural truth of your existence. In contrast, the assumption of separateness from or non-identification with this indivisible Reality that you are is, instead, the very height of presumptuousness, self-inflation, and delusion.

And continue to discriminate: In the relative dimension of the manifest individual soul and the psycho-physical expresssions of personality, you are in relationship to all beings, and to each one. It is incumbent upon you to participate, to cooperate, to love, to give, to receive, to penetrate and to yield, to nurture and to be nurtured, to challenge and to be challenged.

Therefore, you are both Absolute and relative, free of all appearances and identical to them. What you are in and as Consciousness is inherently and eternally non-dependent upon any appearing thing or phenomenon. What you are in and as an essential soul-force of individual being and a psycho-physical personality certainly is dependent upon others and upon the world and its all-creative, all-sustaining, and all-changing Source, Life, God, or Goddess. There are all kinds of discarnate, incarnate, and non-carnate forces, beings, and events that influence and affect you in the manifest dimensions of your soul and personality. But you yourself are precisely the great and only Source, Life, God, or Goddess, because THAT is exactly What you know yourself to Be in your realization of the Fire of the Onlyness of Conscious Life.

If you are going to dare to flash forward into this very realization of Being, then you must dare, forever, here and in the context of whatever other realms or worlds appear, to conform your life and all of life to the truth of this realization. If you love Being so profoundly that you enter into this brilliant realization of It and flash forward into non-separate Unity with each and All, then you must dare to continue to investigate the specific complexion or circumstance of Being that takes the form of your soul-nature and your psycho-physical personality, life, relationships, and environments. And you must dare to express your Being, to live the Fire of the Onlyness of Conscious Life, with fearless integrity in the context of this specific complexion or circumstance of Being that you find from moment to moment, from day to day, from year to year, and from lifetime to lifetime.

There are other things I will write about later, in terms of the progress of this expression when it is essentially untrammeled. It is a most profound Yoga, which I have called "the White-Hot Yoga of the Heart." It is sublime beyond description, but there are nonetheless some very specific things that can be said about it, which may be of use to you in your love, investigation, and expression of the Fire of the Onlyness of Conscious Life. First, however, you must be willing to keep on daring. You must! I can't find another word. I can't pretend to come up with some more diplomatic and tactful way of saying it. Keep daring, and you live. Stop daring, and you die. And the consequences of spiritual suicide in this super-activated evolutionary stage of life are grave indeed.

Are you, or are you not, Consciousness itself?

If Consciousness is What and Who you know your Self to Be, then BE That! Never let anyone talk you out of or otherwise persuade you to abandon your truth! And dare to investigate every fraction of your existence and to conform all of it to the precise dictates of that Fire in your specific and personal case. Do not blithely accept any inherited or conditioned ideology, belief, or structure of action and relationship as necessary or inherently true. Find out what is true for you, precisely and personally. Find out what is necessary and inevitable for your fullest possible expression of the truth of Who you are, the Fire of the Onlyness of Conscious Life that you have realized. And then do that. Keep finding it out again and again, and keep daring again and again, and keep expressing your truth in life, for real, no matter what the consequences in your karmic or previously created relationships and situations.

If you have deeply realized this truth of Being, then the core of what you were before has died. Separateness is now fundamentally and forever dissolved in the essential Heart of your Being. But all of the karmic dimensions of your body, mind, and soul now remain to be utterly conformed to this Heart of Who you are. So if you do not continue to dare to make your freest possible investigation and expression of Being, you will sabotage your realized love of Being. You will concede and compromise, you will wilt into the background of Being where you have lurked for millennia, never before coming forward. And by this Self-betrayal you will reinforce a phantom separateness that for all its insubstantiality will be virtually intractable. You will lay your Self to anxious rest in a tomb of Self-doubt. When will you ever again get up the nerve to dare to Be Who you are?

Therefore, take these suggestions seriously. BE WHO YOU ARE! Be strong! Be brave! Dare! And make the integrity and radical intelligence of this very realization of Being the absolute priority of your entire life. Cultivate above all else the integrity of this process in yourself and everyone you know who values it. Cherish it. Defend it. Do not let it be trampled and smothered by those who are yet trapped in fear and separateness. Nurture it forever and every-where in this human world, and let your ordinary human life and relationships all become free expressions and vehicles of just precisely this greatest priority among all human concerns.

Let us all do these things. Let us each become a supreme adept of this Yoga, so that even if everyone else in all the worlds fell away and ceased to live thus, we would only continue, always, regardless.

These are the kinds of partners I look to find in the Fire of the Onlyness of Conscious Life. I welcome you to join me in the ecstasy of this Burn, now and always, and forever. I love you and I bless you. I hold you to my Heart in inseparable love always, and at the same time I give you absolutely infinite space to BE Who YOU Are. I thrill to your freedom and I bathe in your love, and I thank you with all my Heart for daring to be your Self.

Some Final Statements on My Life and Work, and Where I Take My Stand

F or some time my editors and I assumed that this book would be much more substantial. We intended to include many essays from each of my more primary teaching books, *The White-Hot Yoga of the Heart* and *The Sanctuary of Mutuality*. And we planned for me to conclude the text with an extensive, if summary, autobiography.

At last, we decided to leave out the excerpts from the other books. We felt that the voice of my writing in each of those books is so different from the introductory, summarizing, and welcoming tone of *Waking Down* as it now stands, that working through all that would be confusing and unsatisfying for most readers. I later decided to make a whole book of those excerpts, which will soon be published as *The Perpetual Cosmic Out-of-Court Payoff Machine*.

And, we – mainly I – decided to omit an autobiography, for a number of reasons.

First, you don't really need, and may not even want, to know very much about me. This communication is for you. It does not require a whole lot of personal data about any adept of this Way, not even me, the founding revealer.

Second, while providing an account of my life and the development of my work may be a good thing to do someday, in the final analysis I don't get the clear "Go!" to do so right now. On the contrary, the more I have felt into the prospect of writing such a piece, the more, for many reasons, I feel now is not the appropriate time. Probably it should take the form of a full length book of its own, when there is a significant audience ready and eager to benefit by reading such a thing.

In the meantime, I do feel I should offer you a few key personal communications here at the end of *Waking Down*. I want to offer thanks to some very important people in my life. And I want to remind you again about what this book is and also is not, and to tell you where I take my stand in Being.

Let me begin with a few final salient points that may be of use to you at this initial and exploratory stage of your contact with me.

One is that I have had to make sure that my transmission does not merely lead people to the awakening of divinely human Self-realization. I have had to ensure that it draws them beyond that transition into the full flowering of the second life – which ultimately explodes into and beyond that indescribable apotheosis I call the White Heat. Neither my transmission nor my total Dharma point to some idealized utopian working out of human life in a best possible world. Yes, we will continue to refine identity and relatedness in all kinds of ways, including our endless technological alteration of material and psychic conditions, internal and external. But realizers of conscious embodiment in the second birth should quickly comprehend that this Way is not working toward any kind of earthly paradise that relieves us of the paradox, the ecstatic agony, of being here. Nor is there any ultimately superior place to be in any of the heavenly worlds that are still defined by subject-object relatedness. Waking Down permanently dispels the illusion of potential escape routes. You become that into which you are Waking Down – all of it.

Thus, I have done research and development in my work to guarantee that serious aspirants have the opportunity to burn all the way through into White-Hot presence, here and beyond. One of my essays in *The Sanctuary of Mutuality* is titled, "Ramakrishna on a Hot Tin Roof – or, Why This Present World-Configuration Cannot Possibly Please Us." Ramakrishna was a sublime but mostly disembodied saint of the last century in India. The rest of that title suggests what I'm getting at. The kind of realization that I live, transmit, and teach does not relieve you of problems or make the world OK at last. It resolves you into the fundamental presence it takes to be here with intelligence and at least a little wit – while your very nature effortlessly cooks the world into White-Heatedness, which is neither down, nor up, nor any "where," but simply IS.

Another theme: from time to time someone hotly accuses me of being a guru after all. I have never denied that I am a guru. What I always add, however, is that I am transforming the nature and sociocultural milieu of the guru or adept function. I prefer to use the term "adept" because, whether we like it or not, in our time "guru" has become a four-letter word. If we step back from the details of this or that supposed "guru scandal" and "cult exposé" and look at the larger picture of spiritual life, especially in the West, I think the evidence suggests a bizarre and unfortunate dichotomy.

To summarize, it appears to me that some of the most catalytic accelerators of human evolution are, and have always been, the spiritual transmissions of people in various kinds and degrees of awakening or illumination. But these evolutionary quickeners tend to be disseminated, as they always have been, through some of the most archaic, reactionary sociocultural dynamics on the planet – the monarchic, feudal, and authoritarian hierarchies and often quite totalitarian societies surrounding teachers and teachings.

These approaches aren't working any more. Humanity is insisting on outgrowing them. I am a teacher, an adept – yes, a guru – who is struggling to serve that growth and outgrowing and to cooperate with it fully.

I am also not merely preaching egalitarianism. That's not true mutuality. True mutuality, I observe, notices different degrees of wisdom and experience and has no fundamental problem honoring and utilizing each in his or her own preferred ways. Gurus, adepts, teachers of all kinds really have things to offer!

My work as an adept has evolved over these years. I tell more about that in my other books, especially *The Sanctuary of Mutuality*. As I have indicated here in *Waking Down*, now that other adepts are coming forward to serve aspirants in association with me, I am finding both the necessity and the opportunity to step back into something of a "grandfather position." I am already an elder statesman in this work of healing the core wound and living the Conscious Wound in mutuality.

It's my intention to help open the gateway for the divinely human transformation of all human culture. No one, myself included, can possibly own or control such a cultural sea change. I will certainly continue to steward my own lifework in a vigorous way. I also make room for you and everyone else as best I can. But opening the gateway for a new kind of civilization is not something that someone can do either by himself, or by being cool, calm, and dry.

There are many aspects to my magic, my mysterious effect. One cannot come to have the impact on others that I do without paying serious dues. This is not just a clever rap about consciousness and the body that makes people feel relieved and gets them to hallucinate a fantasy of Self-realization. I am a tantric and a shaman. I don't define these terms the same way that others do, but if you get to know me, you will understand my definitions and my demonstration. I don't own "powers." But I do take responsibility for bringing forth in this world and in all dimensions an inconceivably potent and benign Being-force.

That reality continues to amaze me, yet I cannot afford to ignore it or play it all down. I know my divine archetypes pretty well by now. Though many teachers prefer to say nothing of these sorts of things, I feel that it is crucial for me to indicate to you what they are. I am a direct embodiment of the archetypal energy known as the Remover of Obstacles. Also, the Remover of Doubts. And, the Quickener. And, the Stealer of hearts – though I am always inherently moving to return those hearts with Self-realizing blessing power. Whoever you are, if you find yourself loving me, know that I am loving you too, and that in everything I write, say, or do I am always looking first and foremost to help you love, investigate, and most fully express your true and total Self.

I am an embodiment of the Wish-Fulfiller, or, the Grantor of Boons. I am here to instigate, preside over, and participate mutually in what I sense can be one of the greatest potlatches, or sharing of our total resources, in human history. Sooner or later, I am confident, many people will see these facets of my nature. They will then help make it possible for me to fulfill this portion of my destiny on a great scale.

All these proud and powerful statements are true for me. If you are curious about all this, you'll have to find out for yourself if my life backs up my speech. Yet even as I make these bold statements, which to me are matter-of-fact observations of my effects on others, it is also true that I am full of weakness, fear, and pain. My heart and my very soul have been broken in this lifetime, too.

It pains me beyond measure that I have had to leave two families in order to find myself and activate my greater destiny.

My relationship with my father has never really recovered from my departure into the spiritual quest and especially into the jealous cloister of my Daist years. My relationship with my sister is only now mending from the dislocation we suffered for the same reasons. I am happy I had a few years outside the Daist community with my mother before she died in late 1996. There is no way I can repay my debt to my family, nor heal some of the pain I have caused. So much of who I am has been lovingly shaped and brought forth by who they are and have been. I will always acknowledge and offer my gratitude to them.

I have many regrets with regard to other members of our greater family and also old friends. I wish I had been able to conduct those relationships with more consideration and grace.

148

Many of those individuals are gone now, and there is no recourse.

The other family I had to leave was that of my primary guru, Adi Da, and the men and women with whom I lived and served for nearly two decades. For many reasons, there is no longer any way I can communicate with Adi Da, or even in any real way with most of his devotees. Yet the bonds of love are unbreakable. I wouldn't want to break them. My gratitude, especially to him, and also to the members of his community, never ceases. So I find it painful and sad to know that many of the people I have loved, respected, and revered in my life may well consider me at best a deluded fool.

As for Adi Da himself, I have gone through many shifts and transformations, both in dreams and the waking state, to achieve my necessary autonomy. I don't assume that he is doing anything but blessing me, as always. At the same time, I am well aware that my work stands quite apart from his and will in time present a challenge to many tenets of his teachings, and assumptions on the part of his devotees. I would wish that things might be otherwise. They are not.

Ever since I left my teacher and his community, I have done whatever has appeared necessary to ensure the integrity of, first, my realization and later, my Dharma transmission and adept work. That transmissive service has brought to me and others its own share of heartbreak. My work has always been intense, and many people have found it necessary to take their leave over the years. In most cases this has been a natural and gentle passage, both for them and for me. In some cases it has been quite difficult. I remain saddened by those difficult partings.

To each of you who has gone away from my work and from me confused or hurt, I must say: I am sorry. I wish I could have handled our interchanges in other ways. Please know that I do not take your departure casually. I have considered it deeply and looked for every lesson I could learn that would help me refine my work thereafter. Please also know that I frequently praise you to those who now benefit from these refinements. I remind them that the ease of the way for them has been paved on the roadways you and I had to cut through the jungle of not knowing how to do this, until we could no longer even try to do it together at all.

Thus, I enter the expansive stage of my work with much heaviness in my heart, and certainly no rosy, lighthearted message about the reality of this awakened existence. I am not naive about how difficult it is to bring something this new and revolutionary into the world. As I prepare to publish many books and tapes, and to make a whole new educational and transformational process available to people who are Hungry, I often find myself overwhelmed by the enormity of what I am attempting. Yet I feel I have no choice. I feel shy about stepping forward as I must. I have many trepidations. I don't know who will come to me, and I don't know who will stay with me. I welcome everyone to do what they must and go where they must. But the human consequences of teaching and transmitting as I do are grave, even when only a few are involved. I feel I have no choice. How can I justify withholding this *effective* liberating transmission and wisdom from everyone who is Hungry and deserves the opportunity to respond and receive? I truly have no other choice.

As I begin this new period of my work, I am aware of my debts to quite a number of other people and beings. Many of you have heard from me personally how grateful I am for your presence and your help in my life. If I name some names but not others, some will feel left out. Therefore, I will only mention a very few.

The central core and mystery of my whole awakened life is my relationship to the divine feminine, the goddess. Again, I don't relate to her as others do. My principal way of honoring her is to welcome and invoke her into god-realized, that is to say *conscious and free*, human incarnation as each and every human being. The ones I must, and happily do, honor and acknowledge here in this brief statement are Linda Groves and Fay Fields, both close partners in my life and work. Linda and Fay are among those who have entered into their second births and now function, with me, as awakened adepts. They are goddess-women of rare gifts. Without their presence and aid in my life, what you have before you in this book and my whole White-Hot Way of Mutuality would not be possible. The same is true of many others, but Linda and Fay are special, and I want to acknowledge that.

Again, this book has not been the place to give you all the details of how the White-Hot Way of Mutuality can really become your own. That communication requires other occasions. Similarly, there is a lot more about me that I can tell you in other books, or face to face should we meet someday.

Please remember that, as I wrote in the Prologue, this book is still only a menu, an appetizer at best. There is so much more to be said.

Nonetheless, I can and must close this personal statement by telling you where I take my stand.

Where I take my stand is not in anything I say about my personal life or history, or even about you and the process of transformation we might engage in together and with others.

No, where I take my stand is one place only: *the actual results of my presence and my work in your and others' lives.*

Words never suffice. I can't prove a line of any of this. And I don't care to try.

If you are interested and want to move further in exploring my work for your own purposes, good. Look for results.

Some people take time to begin seeing reliable, tangible effects. I have one friend who worked with me for about two years before he began seeing a remarkable change in himself. As is so often the case, others of us saw the changes in him long before he did. Still, I applaud his skepticism and insistence on tangible results.

I am a somewhat mad and definitely uncommon person, and so are all my close friends – but at the end of the day, none of this is really about me or them. Or, better to say, it is about us only to the extent that it helps you make use of this work for yourself.

Come and do your due diligence with us. Find out if what we are about truly speaks to your heart. Then attend to the simple recommendations other adepts and I make about how to do that due diligence to your satisfaction. And *then*, keep your eyes open for results.

If you do not find anything happening for you, we will certainly support your looking elsewhere. If changes are happening but our particular approach does not feel like a comfortable fit, we'll still support your heading elsewhere for what you need. I have friends who offer a variety of sacred processes quite different from my own. I greatly admire and respect these men and women and would be happy to refer you to them.

Needless to say – but I'll say it anyway – I do hope you can sate your Hunger by Waking Down with my close ones and me right here in our sanctuary of mutuality.

I think that says it. You don't have time to waste. Neither do I. Blessings to you, whoever you are, wherever you go, whenever you find yourself reading these words, and at all other times. May you be blessed to fulfill your divinely human destiny in this and every other lifetime you may inhabit, here in this world and anywhere else!

What to Do Next if You Are Interested

Throughout *Waking Down*, Saniel Bonder refers frequently to his two main teaching books, *The White-Hot Yoga of the Heart: Divinely Human Self-Realization and Sacred Marriage – A Breakthrough Way for "Westerners,"* and, *The Sanctuary of Mutuality: A Waking Maiden Sutra on Embodying the Immortal Nectar of Conscious Love-TRUST*. In the following section, Saniel describes how he invites you to receive these texts.

In addition to publishing Saniel's writings and those of others involved in the White-Hot Way of Mutuality, Mt. Tam Awakenings, Inc., offers workshops, study courses, tape series, and other educational media and events. Our principal workshop, "The Waking Down Weekend," is described below. This section ends with how to contact us for more information.

Receiving Sacred Texts from Saniel

Saniel writes:

"We might view *Waking Down* as the cornerstone for your understanding of what I am offering. Two other texts provide the greater foundation: *The White-Hot Yoga of the Heart* and *The Sanctuary of Mutuality*. These substantial volumes offer extensive advice and reflections for practical application.

"In this manner, I suppose I have come full circle to the way teaching used to be done. The appearance of the printing press and other devices has allowed us to abstract communication from more personal, bodily contexts. Before then, those who held sacred aspirations had to find and cultivate the friendship and face to face help of living teachers. I am planning very soon to publish a selection of excerpts from these longer books, under the title, *The Perpetual Cosmic Out-of-Court Payoff Machine: Selected Essays on the White-Hot Way of Mutuality*. Reading it should give you more of a feeling for whether you would like to acquire the books themselves. If you do, you will then find your way to me.

"I have found that such manuals of practice, outside the context of our actually meeting and exploring a real, sacred relationship together, will tend to be misleading. They will tend to encourage some of the very dissociation that I am trying to help people outgrow. For these reasons, and others, I do not offer *The*

White-Hot Yoga of the Heart or *The Sanctuary of Mutuality* for public sale or distribution. Much more than *Waking Down*, they are my Heart, my person, in book form. In general, I offer them only to those who hunger and yearn enough for what I am presenting to come and meet me face-to-face. As I indicate in Chapter Eleven of *Waking Down*, at that meeting each such person and I make a simple and profound ceremony of exchanging gifts.

"For those who are attracted, but who live at great distance or are otherwise prohibited from physically coming to meet me: let my friends and me know what your situation is. If, after reading this book or otherwise becoming acquainted with my work, you know you want these other teaching texts, we can work out the details by mail or by phone. I don't want to disqualify you by virtue of geographic or other complications. Even so, it is still true that you will have to make bodily contact with me or other adepts of this approach if you wish to do the work to the fullest."

The Waking Down Weekend

The Waking Down Weekend is a three day intensive that explores very deeply and personally the topics introduced in this book. This is a place to begin Waking Down into your Self-realization – we won't just be talking about it. Here, your awakening process will likely come alive with a surprising intensity. During the weekend you will spend several hours with Saniel and work with a group of awakened adept-facilitators who, along with Saniel, offer a catalytic transmission of Being-force. In extensive small group meetings you'll experience the breakthrough of mutuality and how it revolutionizes the spiritual journey.

Please contact us for more information.

How to Reach Us

For more information on books by Saniel Bonder in both print and unabridged audiotape formats, on workshops, and on other publications and offerings by Mt. Tam Awakenings, Inc., we invite you to contact us:

· Call us toll-free at 888-741-5000
· Fax a note to us at 415-721-0111
· Check out our web site at www.sanielbonder.com
· Send e-mail to info@sanielbonder.com

We look forward to hearing from you.

Notes

Notes

Notes

Notes

Notes

Notes